The
MIDDLE
SIZED
Church

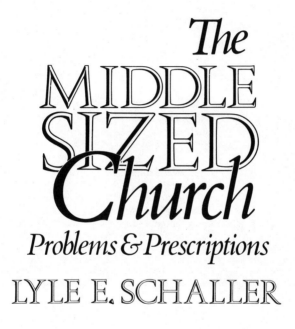

The MIDDLE SIZED Church

Problems & Prescriptions

LYLE E. SCHALLER

Abingdon Press

Nashville

The Middle-Sized Church
Problems and Prescriptions
Copyright © 1985 by Abingdon Press

Seventh Printing 1992

This book is printed on recycled, acid-free paper.

Library of Congress Cataloging in Publication Data

SCHALLER, LYLE E.
  The middle-sized church.
  Companion volume to the author's The multiple staff and the larger church and The small church is different.
  Bibliography: p.
  1. Church management. I. Title
BV652.S326   1985   254   84-12496

ISBN 0-687-26948-2

Contents

Preface

On an average Sunday morning approximately thirty million adults, age eighteen and over, will attend worship in a Protestant church in the United States. Nearly one-third of them will be present in congregations in which the average attendance is under 100, slightly over 30 percent will worship with congregations in which the attendance averages between 100 and 200, and approximately 38 percent will worship in Protestant churches that average more than 200 at worship. This book is directed to the leaders in that middle third, the churches averaging between 100 and 200 at worship. One congregation out of every five fits into that category. In other words, the one-fourth of all Protestant congregations that are identified here as "middle-sized" account for approximately 31 percent of all Protestant churchgoers on the average Sunday. In Canada this bracket probably includes at least one-fourth of all Protestant churches and at least 40 percent of all Protestant churchgoers on the average Sunday.

The distinctive characteristic of these churches, however, is not the common denominator of size. That is a convenient way to categorize them, but knowing the size of these congregations tells us little. A far more useful conceptual framework is to focus on the congregational culture, the distinctive personality and the internal dynamics.

In the New York City headquarters of the American Telephone and Telegraph Company hangs a picture of Angus

McDonald, a nineteenth-century lineman struggling in the face of a blizzard to keep the telephone lines open. That print symbolizes a central element of the corporate culture of the Bell System. For 107 years the primary focus was not on the organizational structure of the corporation or on a strategy for marketing, but on service. This incredibly strong service ethic influenced the structure of the corporation, determined the kind of people the company sought as new employees, guided the development of the internal reward system, and enabled employees to have a remarkable loyalty to "Ma Bell."

The congregational culture may be the best beginning point for gaining an understanding of the distinctive personality of a middle-sized church. This is the theme of the first chapter.

The congregational culture also may be the key to explaining why middle-sized churches differ so much from one another. This is the focus of the second chapter. A variety of different congregations are identified to illustrate the basic point that no two are alike.

The small congregation often resembles a family while the very large churches frequently are built around the professional staff and the organizational structure. The volunteer lay leadership comes and goes, usually with only a modest degree of visibility. By contrast, individual personalities tend to stand out more clearly in the middle-sized church. Six familiar personalities are identified in the third chapter to illustrate this point.

From this observer's experiences with hundreds of middle-sized churches one of the most widely shared characteristics is a poor self-image. This low esteem causes too many congregational leaders to plan and make decisions on the assumption, "This really is just a small church." The fourth chapter is devoted to that issue.

As a group the pastors with the highest level of frustration, fatigue, and guilt may be those serving congregations averaging between 160 and 240 at Sunday morning worship. Those often are earned feelings and the dilemma of the awkward-sized church is the theme of the fifth chapter.

The longest inflationary cycle in history has made conventional wisdom obsolete in many areas of life. One that has been seriously neglected, but is of fundamental importance to the churches, is that the congregation relying exclusively on the unified budget often will be seriously underfinanced. This is the central thesis of the final chapter, which also offers some alternative proposals for expanding the financial base of the church.

This is the final volume in what could be described as a trilogy that is based on the assumption that the size of the congregation, as measured by the average attendance at Sunday morning worship, is a useful conceptual framework for analyzing Protestant churches. The first of the three, *The Multiple Staff and the Larger Church,* was published in 1980. The second, *The Small Church Is Different!* was published two years later. This volume completes that series.

In a world filled with computers and electronic word processors, readers occasionally inquire how a particular volume was composed. Thanks to the wonders of modern technology the task of this writer was facilitated by the use of a kit that includes a word processor that is fluent in every known written language, has only one moving part, uses no electricity, offers variable margins, does not give off any detectable degree of radiation, required absolutely no maintenance, is user-friendly, readily produces an endless variety of graphics, is almost completely silent in operation, is easily portable, and is widely available at an unbelievably low price. The complete kit, consisting of a dozen ball-point pens and four yellow pads, is available in thousands of retail stores.

This book is dedicated to five friends of many years who share my feelings about the centrality of the worshiping congregation as the institutional expression of the Christian church.

Lyle E. Schaller
Yokefellow Institute
Richmond, Indiana

CHAPTER ONE

What Is the Middle-Sized Church?

To a substantial degree the middle-sized church can be described by how it differs from both large and small congregations. Usually it is seen as too large to share a minister with another congregation, but too small to have two ministers. It is too large for the members to be satisfied with the limited scale program typical of the small church, but too small to offer the broad range of programming, especially for youth, that some of the newer members expect. It often is too large to expect the minister to function without the assistance of at least a part-time secretary, but rarely provides the pastor with the help of a full-time secretary. It usually is too small for the leaders to agree the congregation needs a full-scale systematic new member enlistment effort, but too large for enough new members to come in on their own initiative to offset the inevitable attrition.

Frequently the leaders of the middle-sized congregation are convinced it is too large to do without an organized choir, but the members often see it as too small to afford the help of a paid choir director. It is too large to function simply as "one big family," but too small for the leaders to see an obvious need for regularly expanding the group life. Most middle-sized churches are too large for the governing board to serve as "the committee of the whole" and to be responsible for all facets of congregational life from finances to Christian education to evangelism to real estate to missions, but too small for everyone to be comfortable with an elaborate organizational structure that includes a variety of standing committees and short-term task forces that meet ten to fifteen times annually. It is large enough to include a strong and well-organized women's organization, but usually too small for a men's fellowship to survive.

Many of the middle-sized churches are too large to include both seventh-graders and twelfth-graders in the same youth group, but frequently their leaders believe they are too small to have one youth group for senior high youth and a separate organization for junior high students.

Typically the middle-sized congregation is too large to be shock-free from a change of ministers and/or a long vacancy in the pulpit, but too small to expect the typical pastorate to be *at least* ten years in length or to bring in an intentional interim pastor on a full-time basis during the vacancy period.

Frequently the middle-sized congregation sees itself as too small to afford even part-time paid staff specialists in music, youth ministries, bookkeeping, or children's work, but too large to expect competent volunteers to always be available and willing to carry those responsibilities. It is large enough to benefit from electronic data processing of membership and financial records but too small for the leaders to agree they need a computer.

Most of the members of the middle-sized congregation know it is small enough so everyone should know everyone else by name, but frequently it is really too large to realistically expect everyone to call everyone else by name, and it is too small for most members to affirm the advantages of everyone wearing a name tag.

While this will vary greatly according to denominational polity, and especially by race, the typical middle-sized congregation is too small for the lay leaders to concede that "the minister is in charge around here," but too large for lay volunteers to be able to allocate the necessary time every week for it to be lay-controlled (as is the pattern in most small churches).

A substantial majority of all middle-sized congregations are located in communities in which at least one-third of the residents do not have any active church affiliation. The typical middle-sized church is large enough to offer a ministry to meet the needs of many of the unchurched, but most of the members are convinced that their congregation is too small to have sufficient resources to launch a major effort to reach the unchurched.

Many middle-sized congregations, including most of those in urban communities, are too large for the grapevine to be a reliable communication channel between the church and the members, but frequently they do not believe the time, energy, and money required for a weekly newsletter can be justified.

Responding to These Paradoxes

When taken together these introductory comments reveal one of the distinctive characteristics of the middle-sized congregation. The leader of the middle-sized congregation usually will respond to this series of paradoxical statements with varied comments.

"Yes, that describes us all right! I'm sorry to admit it, but those statements reflect our limitations and shortcomings. We are kind of powerless to do all that God wants us to do, and sometimes I feel guilty about that."

"You've identified our problems all right. Now what advice do you have for us on how we can respond to those problems?"

These first two responses illustrate feelings of guilt, inadequacy, a strong problem-orientation, powerlessness, and frustration.

By contrast, many of the leaders of small-member churches respond with a different reaction to comments about the limitations of their congregation by, "Well, after all, what can you expect of us? We're simply a small church trying to survive and we're surviving." The translation of that is it is very difficult to make any individual or organization that is functioning around survival goals feel guilty about trying to survive. Survival is a basic drive for both human beings and institutions. (The smallest denomination in American Protestantism, the Evangelical Lutheran Church in America [Eielsen Synod], founded in 1846, was still alive in 1984, although down to only two congregations and fewer than 100 members. More than a score of denominations include fewer than 30 churches.)

At the other extreme the leaders of the large membership churches, when confronted with an inconsistency or inadequacy in the program, ministry, or outreach, are far more likely to respond, "Well, let's do something about it. We have the resources to correct that, so let's get to it."

In other words, there is a tendency in the middle-sized parish to focus on problems, limitations, liabilities, and shortcomings and to allow those to dominate the agenda. This often produces feelings of guilt, a sense of powerlessness, and frustration that can immobilize the middle-sized congregation.

A far more productive response to this introductory series of paradoxical statements about the middle-sized church would be something like this:

"That's a dumb way to begin the first chapter of a book about the middle-sized church! Instead of reinforcing our feelings of guilt and our sense of inadequacy, why didn't you begin your book by identifying the strengths, the unique assets, and the positive characteristics of the middle-sized congregation? I suppose you'll say you began with those paradoxical statements to make the reader believe this is a book about 'my congregation' and to prove that you do have a firsthand understanding of the distinctive characteristics of the middle-sized congregation, but I think it would have been better to identify and affirm the unique assets of the middle-sized church and to suggest ways those assets can be used to strengthen, reinforce, and expand the outreach of that church."

That could be a useful introductory section for a book on the middle-sized church, but these paradoxical statements also provide an introduction to the most distinctive characteristic of that one-fourth of Protestant congregations on this continent that average between 100 and 200 at worship on Sunday morning.

While those who have had an intimate association with a middle-sized church almost certainly will recognize at least some of these paradoxical statements, to conceptualize the middle-sized congregation as a paradox is a great oversimplification. It is a far more complex order of creation than simply a bundle of paradoxes. Perhaps the most distinctive characteristic of the middle-sized church is that no two are alike. It is relatively easy to find many similarities among smaller congregations. Frequently, for example, the 70-member congregation located in a residential neighborhood in a large city will have much in common with the 75-member church meeting in a building out in the open country and also with the 70-member church located on the north side of the small county seat town.

Likewise the senior minister of the 2700-member Baptist church in Alabama often will be surprised at how much he shares in common with the senior pastor of the 2500-member Lutheran parish in Minneapolis or the senior pastor of the 2900-member Methodist church in Florida or the senior minister of the 2600-member Presbyterian church in Pittsburgh.

By contrast, middle-sized churches' experiences often differ greatly from one another, even from within the same denominational family. Frequently about the only point of commonality is size. One small-town congregation that averages 175 at worship on Sunday morning is served by a minister who is also a student at a seminary 70 miles away, while in a nearby city a congregation with an average of 165 at worship has two full-time ordained ministers. One 300-member church has an annual budget of $29,000 and in another 300-member congregation the members contributed nearly $165,000 last year. Some of these differences among the churches in this broad-size category are explored in subsequent pages, but first it may help to discuss a second concept that may explain the unique character of the middle-sized church.

The key to understanding the distinctive personality, role, ministry, and future of the middle-sized parish is not to begin with paradoxes or strengths or problems or community setting, but to reflect on the congregational culture. That may be why middle-sized churches differ so much from one another.

The Sources of a Concept

Back in 1979 Michael Rutter published his study of twelve inner city schools in London.[1] As he studied a school's sense of purpose and commitment, he identified thirty-nine measurable characteristics that were found in what he concluded were the best secondary schools. These schools had better than anticipated records—given the background, academic histories, and disciplinary problems of the incoming students—on attendance, orderliness, and scholastic achievement. The principals laid down clear guidelines for the teachers to follow and monitored their compliance. This included the assignment of considerable amounts of homework on a regular basis and an overall expectation of high performance by the students. The teachers gave praise when it was earned and frequently excellent work was posted on bulletin boards or in the corridors. Rutter used the Greek term *ethos* to identify the basic qualities he concluded were more important in fostering a productive learning climate.

Fifteen years earlier Professors Roger G. Barker and Paul V. Gump published their landmark volume *Big School, Small*

School.[2] In this study of public high schools in eastern Kansas the authors used the term "behavior setting" to describe the school environment and its impact on the students. The behavior setting includes the size of the school, afterschool meetings, happenings on the school bus, the interaction between teachers and students, the continuity of relationships, social values, class size, participation in extracurricular activities, and a host of other variables.

In recent years scores of studies have been published reporting on the influence of the educational cultures of public and private schools and the impact of the school culture on student behavior and achievement.[3]

More recently the publication of the best-selling book ever written on American business, *In Search of Excellence,*[4] has popularized the concept of a corporate culture. The authors studied some of what they considered to be the best-managed corporations in the nation and identified core characteristics that were common to all. These include what they described as "a bias for action," "hands-on, value-driven" (decide what your company stands for and work hard to reinforce those values), "stick to the knitting" (emphasize what you know and do best), "close to the consumer" (an obsession to be oriented to the client), and a capability for "managing ambiguity and paradox."

It was pointed out in the opening pages of this chapter that the middle-sized church is a bundle of paradoxes. The ability to understand, accept, and enjoy ambiguity may be one of the most important characteristics of the happy and effective pastor of the middle-sized congregation. That ambiguity is a product of the congregational culture of the middle-sized churches.

The central thesis of this book is that the middle-sized church is not simply a bundle of paradoxes; each congregation has its own distinctive *ethos* or behavior setting or culture and that explains why no two are alike. To understand the internal dynamics of the typical middle-sized congregation, it is essential to accept the fact that each congregation really represents a distinctive culture.

In one congregation the culture expects every member to be in church every Sunday morning, on Sunday evening, and also on Wednesday evening. Most of the members respond by being present. In another congregation, in the same community with its meeting place less than a block away and with the same number of members, the congregational culture projects a different set of expectations. In the typical month one-half of the members never attend Sunday morning worship, one-fourth are present three or four Sundays out of the month, and another quarter attend once or twice a month. One of two brothers who grew up in the same home is now a member of the first congregation and rarely misses any of the three services held each week. The other brother, who is a member of the second congregation, attends perhaps a dozen times a year. The *ethos* or the behavior setting or the congregational culture is a self-selecting factor in determining who joins which congregation and also explains how people behave after they unite with that congregation. This can be illustrated by the behavior of the person who was an irregular participant for years in one congregation and today, after accompanying his or her spouse to another church, is now a remarkably active member of that second parish. While we need to be careful to avoid simplistic single-factor analysis, it would be equally naive to overlook the impact of the congregational culture on the members' behavior patterns as well as on their belief systems.

In some churches the congregational culture explains why the largest attendance of the year is on Christmas Eve while in many the culture produces the greatest attendance on Easter and in others the congregational culture explains why the biggest crowd is on Mother's Day or on Homecoming Sunday when the anniversary of the founding of that congregation is celebrated.

The culture also explains why in one congregation a

18

layperson serves as president of the congregation, but in another the minister fills that role.

The culture is a factor in the reason why some congregations gain the reputation as "preacher-killers," while others earn a reputation as "a great place to serve."

An understanding of the culture will help us see why in one congregation Sunday school attendance usually exceeds worship attendance on the typical Sunday morning by a three-to-two margin while in another church of the same size the worship attendance is four times as large as Sunday school attendance.

The congregational culture helps us understand why one church is organized around missions and outreach while in another parish nearly all the resources are allocated to the care of the members.

At this point someone may object, "But you're simply trying to inject a fancy term for what we've always simply called 'tradition.'" There is some truth to that statement, but it oversimplifies. The culture does include traditions, customs, and habits, but the culture is a larger and more inclusive concept. The culture is why those traditions and customs endure. The culture or the ethos is why individuals behave according to one pattern while members of one congregation, but change their behavior patterns after transferring their membership to another congregation. The culture influences which traditions are upheld and which can be discarded. The congregational culture also helps us understand why no two middle-sized churches are carbon copies of each other.

Our Culture Makes Us Different

"This congregation was organized back in 1907," recalled the pastor of what is now clearly a suburban church. "This was a completely rural county until the mid-sixties, when the migration from the city and the older suburbs brought a lot of younger families out here. Lower land prices meant the prices of new houses were several thousand dollars less than in the urban counties. For its first fifty years or so, this was a rural congregation and I doubt if it ever had more than 75 people in either Sunday school or worship. One of the old-timers told me they used to have close to a hundred for Easter, but I don't see how they could have squeezed that many into that old building. My predecessor came in 1969 as the first full-time minister. During the nine years he was there, they built a new parsonage and a four-room educational wing. They also purchased four acres next to the property from a member who was getting ready to subdivide his farm. By the time I came, they were planning to build a new sanctuary; this was completed during my third year. As soon as we get that paid for, we're planning to build a fellowship hall, but that's still a few years away. We need it right now, but we can't afford it until we get more of that high interest mortgage paid off."

"What's your average attendance?" inquired the visitor.

"We average 160 in Sunday school and close to 175 at worship, and that just about fills our new sanctuary. We really need to go to two services, but I doubt if I could get a dozen votes for that if we brought it up at a congregational meeting. We're crowded, but that's not the real issue here. My basic problem is I serve four congregations. First of all, there're still about 60 old-timers here who were members twenty years ago or more back when this was a rural church with a part-time minister. Second, there are the folks who consti- tuted that first wave of newcomers. I call them the new old-timers. Most of my opposition to change comes from them. Most of them joined either before my predecessor came or during the first couple of years of his pastorate. Among other things they are pretty clear they prefer to be part of a small church and a lot of them resent the recent growth. These are the folks who have been most opposed to my suggestion to get a full-time church secretary. My predecessor's wife acted as a volunteer church secretary so they can't understand why a small church like this needs a full-time church secretary. Some of them think that the idea of a two-day-a-week secretary is a luxury.

"The third congregation is the old newcomers. They joined during the last several years of my predecessor's tenure and my first couple of years here. Many of them spearheaded the effort to build the new sanctuary.

"The new newcomers are the folks who came since we moved into the new sanctuary. They have no firsthand knowledge of how it was to worship in the old building. We've converted the upstairs into a youth room and the basement still serves as our fellowship hall."

"Who are you in this setting?" inquired the visitor.

"There are two answers to that question," replied the pastor. "In general terms, I'm an old newcomer. If you want to be more precise, I am *the* pastor to the new newcomers, a friend to the old newcomers, an intruder or trespasser for many of the new old-timers who are still strongly attached to my predecessor and, finally, the preacher, but not an influential leader for some of the old old-timers. Several of the old old-timers see me as a city slicker. Those are the ones who keep reminding me that my predecessor was born and reared on a farm while my father taught school in Chicago most of his life, and I grew up in the city."

This remarkably astute analysis offers an introduction to the concept of why middle-sized churches tend to differ so much from one another. About all they have in common is their size. Their differences can best be understood not by looking at the denominational affiliation, but rather by understanding the concept of congregational culture. This concept of a congregational culture also helps us understand both why today's congregation may be substantially different from the same congregation meeting in that same building a generation earlier and completely unlike a similar-size church a block away.

This basic point can be illustrated by a quick look at seven congregations, each averaging between 140 and 150 at Sunday morning worship, each one served by a full-time resident minister, and all seven affiliated with the same denominational family. One is a seventeen-year-old Korean congregation. Another is the largest Protestant congregation in a small midwestern town. The third is located two blocks from what is now the heart of the central business district of a large city and once it was the largest church of its denomination in the state. The fourth is a black congregation in Alabama. The fifth is a three-year-old Anglo suburban church in Minnesota. The sixth is a Mexican-American congregation in Los Angeles County. The seventh is a racially integrated congregation in Kansas City which meets in a building that once housed one of the most prestigious white churches in that city. These seven congregations are about the same size, if size is measured by the average attendance at worship on Sunday morning, but they vary in membership from 655 in that old downtown church to 135 in that three-year-old suburban church in Minnesota. Each one has its own pastor, but in two cases the pastor has a part-time secular job while another pastor is assisted by a half-time retired minister of visitation and a fourth has the assistance of a seminary intern who is full-time for ten months of the year.

These congregations also illustrate another aspect of the congregational culture that can be summarized by a word that is widely used in political campaigns, football games, and physics laboratories. The word is momentum. The congregation meeting in a large building two blocks from the heart of the central business district once averaged over 650 at worship, but is now down to 145. The long-time leaders feel their church has lost its momentum and is caught in the throes of inevitable decline. The three-year-old new mission in Minnesota doubled its worship attendance from 70 to 140 and the leaders are convinced momentum is on their side.

Momentum is one reason that the numerically growing congregation tends to be more receptive to innovation, less bound by tradition, more open to maverick leaders, and more attractive to upwardly mobile persons.[5]

When the focus is on the middle-sized church, the congregational culture, rather than the denominational affiliation or the educational training of the minister or the size or the ethnic background of the members or age or the location of the meeting place, becomes the most important single factor in understanding the internal dynamics of congregational life. This central point can be explained first by a brief case study and subsequently by further elaboration of the concept of a congregational culture.

What Is the Congregational Culture?

"Today people want to know how the biblical faith relates to current issues! What does the Bible say about abortion or nuclear weapons or bringing up children or helping the poor or how we respond to the growing numbers of the elderly or to the end of the world? If we're really serious about reaching the young adults of today, we need a Sunday school class that will focus on those kinds of issues," proclaimed the fifty-six-year-old Steve Baker, one of the most outspoken members of the Christian education committee at the 420-member Woodlawn Church. "I believe we need a discussion-type class that looks at the issues younger people are thinking about. It should have a leader who is skilled at stimulating discussion and meet in a room that encourages people to participate, rather than to sit and be talked at by the teacher."

"That sounds like a good idea to me and I believe we should give it a try," added Pat Butler, "but where would we have them meet? The parlor is the only room we have that really lends itself to that type of class."

"That's the real issue," agreed Kim Evans. "I agree with the idea and the parlor is the logical room for such a class, but I doubt if the Fifty-Fifty Class will be interested in finding another place to meet. They've been meeting in the parlor for at least twenty years now. If I remember correctly, the Fifty-Fifty Class and the women's fellowship got together and paid the full cost of redecorating the parlor about ten or twelve years ago. That room is filled with their furniture and the walls are covered with pictures of past leaders from both the women's organization and the Fifty-Fifty Class. Both of the sofas and at least five of those big easy chairs represent memorials to deceased members."

"You doubt they will give up that room?" bellowed Marty Phillips. "I *know* they won't give it up!"

"Well, as you all know, my wife and I are members of the Fifty-Fifty Class," explained Steve Baker, "and I've been telling those folks that if they would get behind a building program, we could have our own room in the new addition. Some of us have been arguing for twenty years or longer that we need to build an educational wing on the east side of the building. Everyone agrees we need it, but no one seems willing to take the bull by the horns and go ahead with it."

"I'm all in favor of trying to start a new young adult class," declared Jan Halstead. "The class I'm in is the youngest of any of our adult classes, and most of us are past forty, but I'm not sure I agree with the idea of organizing it around a discussion of controversial issues. Why couldn't we simply let it be a Bible study class for younger adults? I'm afraid a lot of our members may be upset if we try to organize an issue-centered class. That may cause more turmoil than we're prepared for."

"But that's my point," interrupted Steve Baker. "This congregation has been so wishy-washy on issues and so afraid of controversy for so long that our community image resembles a bowl of cold oatmeal. Today's younger generation grew up in the controversial sixties. They're not afraid of issues. They're used to controversy! Look at how many out of that generation are living together without benefit of clergy. I've got a daughter who's been living with this fellow for three years now and they say that someday they may get married. This church has to recognize it's a new world out there. If we don't, we'll sit around here, grow old together, and one day close when we run out of members."

"I know what you mean about the Fifty-Fifty Class' attachment to the parlor," sighed Terry Wheeler. "We could use the Open Circle's classroom for this new class if we decide to go ahead with it. The folks in the Open Circle Class are very cooperative and I think we could use their room. They would meet out in the corridor if we told them that's all that is available. Their room is not as nice for a discussion class as the parlor, but I believe it's our only alternative."

"I'm with Jan," added the sixty-three-year-old Martha Dyer. "I would like to see a new class for young adults, but I don't believe we should split the church in the process of starting it. Why don't we table this for now and go on to the next item on the agenda and come back to this next month when our minister can be here. He'll be back from vacation on Friday, and I don't think we should do anything until we've heard what he has to say."

This discussion illustrates a concept that can be a useful beginning point in looking at a variety of points, but it is especially significant when the subject is the middle-sized congregation. That concept is that each congregation, in addition to its religious belief system, also has its own distinctive organizational culture.

An overly simplistic definition of the congregational culture would be the shared value system. What values do the members share, seek to uphold and reinforce, try to perpetuate, and perhaps even share with those outside that culture? A more adequate definition can be offered by identifying eight different aspects of a congregational culture that were illustrated by the discusion over organizing a new adult Sunday school class at the Woodlawn Church.

First, and perhaps central to any discussion of a congregational culture, is the system of shared values. At Woodlawn one of those widely shared values is the importance of the Sunday school. While there was a clear difference of opinion on the best approach to organizing a new adult class, no one even suggested that adult classes were obsolete or not important. These members, by their presence and active participation, also affirmed the value of the Christian education committee. Later on we will examine a variety of other shared values in the middle-sized church as well as other aspects of the congregational culture.

A second component of a culture is a clear understanding of "how we do things around here." At Woodlawn that first was illustrated by a recognition that the Fifty-Fifty Class controlled the use of the parlor on Sunday morning. Subsequently, Martha Dyer reminded the other committee members that around here we do not make any major changes without first giving the minister a chance to be heard. She did not suggest the minister would be heeded, but in the typical middle-sized church the minister at least is accorded the opportunity to voice an opinion. By contrast, in thousands of long-established huge churches the congregational culture makes it clear to everyone that only rarely do suggestions for changes emanate from anyone except the ministerial staff. In the middle-sized church the minister often suggests creative new ideas to a layperson, hoping that person will introduce the idea at the appropriate meeting. In the huge churches creative laypeople suggest new ideas to a staff member, hoping that paid staff person will introduce that idea at the appropriate meeting. These behavioral norms constitute a critical element of the congregational culture of the middle-sized church. They range from the age of first Communion for children to the garb for the choir to the schedule for Christmas Eve to who returns thanks before eating at the monthly potluck to who is permitted to play the organ.

A third part of the congregational culture, and one that will receive considerable attention both here and in subsequent chapters because it is such an influential factor in how middle-sized congregations actually function, is the organizational structure. What is the organizational structure for planning and decision-making? How is it constituted? What values and goals are the foundation blocks for that organizational structure?

From the discussion at Woodlawn Church, it appears the Christian education committee (*a*) has the authority to organize a new class, subject to hearing from the minister, (*b*) does not have the authority to designate which rooms will be used by the various classes, or at least does not control use of the parlor, and (*c*) does not have the authority to initiate a building program. One of the most crucial factors in determining how open a congregation is to innovation is clarity on (*a*) who holds the authority to allocate scarce resources among competng demands and (*b*) who has the authority to initiate new ideas and changes. A lack of clarity on those two points of authority normally creates an organizational bias against innovation, in favor of the status quo, against action and in favor of institutional maintenance over outreach. In the best churches that organizational bias is for action, not continued passivity, and for the making of the necessary decisions, not for "passing the buck."

While many people are reluctant to think in these terms, a very influential part of the congregational culture is the system of rewards and punishments. What are the control systems? If the Fifty-Fifty Class completely ignores the Christian education committee's efforts to start a new discussion format class for young adults, will the Fifty-Fifty Class be (*a*) rewarded by being allowed to use the parlor or (*b*) be punished by being moved to another room? Will the Christian education committee "punish" inflexibility by leaving the Fifty-Fifty Class alone and "reward" flexibility and cooperative spirit by asking the Open Circle Class to give up its classroom and meet in the corridor? Those may be exaggerated comments but they do reflect the fact that in every congregation a control system is in operation which represents a fourth component of the congregational culture.

A fifth slice of the congregational culture cuts across all the other layers and can be summarized in one word, *interaction*. How do the shared values and belief systems interact with the organizational structure, with the people, with the reward and punishment systems, and with the leaders to influence what happens?

The conversation at Woodlawn Church, and especially that categorical statement by Marty Phillips, suggests the Christian education committee is not prepared to challenge the Fifty-Fifty Class for use of the parlor on Sunday morning. When the strongly held and widely shared value of creating a new class comes into conflict with the behavioral norm that states the Fifty-Fifty Class has control of the parlor, nearly everyone recognizes this could produce a traumatic confrontation. While it is not absolutely clear from this part of the conversation, it appears that avoiding confrontations is a more strongly held value of this congregational culture than organizing a new adult class.

A sixth facet of the congregational culture that distinguishes the middle-sized congregation from the small church is turf. In the smaller churches the members resemble a family. The door to the kitchen is never locked in the home of the typical family. In the small church the kitchen is not only a place to prepare meals, it also may be the place for a Sunday school class to meet, the site for a social period following the monthly Board meeting or between Sunday school and worship, and it may even serve as the bride's room before a wedding. In the middle-sized church turf begins to become more important. The minister expresses the need for a private office; instead of one room without a label on the door, there are two rooms, one labeled "men" and one "women"; the women, who paid for the renovation of the parlor, display no hesitation in prohibiting anyone with food or beverages from entering that sacred place; and the Fifty-Fifty Class is not about to surrender its turf to some new and probably irresponsible or possibly even subversive new class!

A seventh component of the congregational culture was

identified in this example as the pictures on the walls of the parlor and the furniture given as memorials. What the stranger sees as photographs, banners, sofas, chairs, tables, and furnishings for that room, the members of the Fifty-Fifty Class see as part of their identity. Those furnishings symbolize the tribal legends, represent visible reminders of the heritage, affirm the tribe's right to that place, and reinforce their sense of being part of a continuing fellowship.

This aspect of congregational culture can be seen most clearly when one congregation sells its meeting place to a different religious group. The sellers carry these treasures away with them and install them in their new meeting place. The buyers bring their symbols, pictures, mementos, books, banners, chairs, and other furnishings with them and quickly turn that strange building into "our new church home."

Finally, of course, the people constitute the heart of the congregational culture. Sometimes the members are described as "friendly" or "old" or "enthusiastic" or "spirit-filled" or "worried" or "preacher-killers" or "mission-minded," but those words tend to ignore the fact that the members not only create but are a product of the congregational culture. It is a rash and misleading oversimplification to talk about the members without reference to that congregation's distinctive culture. The culture at Woodlawn Church appears to have encouraged these members to speak freely within the confines of the Christian education committee, but to be cautious about going ahead with changes that others might question or oppose. To varying degrees we are all captives of the culture in which we live and the local church constitutes a culture that influences the behavior of its members.

One of the basic assumptions on which this book is based is that the size of the congregation affects the culture; therefore the middle-sized church provides a distinctively different culture than does the small congregation or the large church. The impact of the culture on the middle-sized church is what makes it a distinctive, perhaps a unique, category of congregations.

In the best of the churches, the leaders have created, sometimes over a period of several generations, a rich tapestry of symbols, parables, folk sayings, favorite expressions, beliefs, legends, stories, rituals, customs, and festivals which reinforce the feeling that indeed this is a unique congregation. By contrast, the weak churches are swathed in layers of gray cloth—ready for their funeral. The congregational culture gives meaning to life for many of the members.

This concept of an institutional culture also can be illustrated by reflecting briefly on the impact of the denominational culture on the clergy. From this writer's experience it appears the denominational culture of the Lutheran Church in America encourages pastors to focus on nurture while in The United Methodist Church the denominational culture causes ministers to spend more time thinking about career and compensation. In the Episcopal Church the denominational culture places a greater emphasis on liturgy and the sacraments while in the Lutheran Church—Missouri Synod the denominational culture places education high on the pastoral list of priorities and in the Southern Baptist Convention the denominational culture encourages pastors to choose between "orthodoxy" and missions as the number one issue. The culture of the Presbyterian Church (U.S.A.) has yet to be fully formed, but competing for the attention of ministers are biblical interpretation, social justice, evangelism, and denominational loyalty.

Conflict out of Culture

One of the more common sources of lay-clergy conflict is when the minister comes from a religious culture that overlaps only slightly with the congregational culture of the church that pastor is now serving. One example is the United Methodist minister who was born and reared in rural America, spent thirty years serving rural churches, and recently was appointed to serve a twenty-five-year-old upper-class suburban church in which many of the members spend more time at the country club than in church. Another is the allegation that three or four years in a university-related theological seminary may prepare a student for entrance into a doctoral program, but not for the parish ministry. A third example is the minister born in 1947, who learned the reason the federal government minted coins in a circular shape is so they will roll, who comes to a congregation served by lay leaders who clearly remember the Great Depression and know the reason money is flat on both sides is to make it easier to stack.

A fourth example of this type of conflict is between the veteran minister who enjoyed three long and happy pastorates leading congregations through very successful building programs and the leaders of his present congregation who were born after World War II and possess a strong mission orientation and little interest in constructing new buildings or in paying off mortgages.

Perhaps the most common three-way source of conflict in the middle-sized congregation surfaces when the long-time members assume the primary responsibility of the minister is to be a shepherd and to devote substantial time to the members on a one-to-one basis, the new members are convinced the minister should work with the appropriate committees on program development and administration while the new pastor places a high value on evangelism, new member enlistment, and the concept of the minister as an enabler with people rather than as a professional staff person for committees.

Another expression of the three-way conflict that arises from contrasting congregational cultures often is found in the long-established congregation that doubles or triples in size within several years following the arrival of the new minister. On the surface, the issue appears to be the leadership style of the pastor. The old-timers, who spent decades living with, learning and expressing the concept "this is a small church that is owned and operated by the laity," are distressed by the aggressive and, at times, unilateral leadership style of the minister. The first wave of new members like, respect, and support the pastor, but they are convinced "this church needs a collegial style of decision-making and our pastor often ignores the leaders and plunges on without consulting us." The newest members explain that one of the reasons they joined is: "We like a pastor who is willing to lead, to lift up a vision of new challenges, and to turn that vision into reality. Where we were before, we had ministers who wanted to be enablers rather than leaders. We like it here."

Each of these groups of members is evaluating the leadership role and style of the pastor from a different culture.

The congregational culture not only helps explain some of the sources of conflict, it also provides the context for examining the differences among churches. This can be illustrated by looking at several contrasting categories of middle-sized congregations.

CHAPTER
TWO

No Two Are Alike!

Perhaps the most productive beginning point for anyone seeking to understand the middle-sized Protestant church on the North American continent is to accept the fact that no two are exactly alike. They range from the big frog in the small town to the Spirit-filled charismatic fellowship to the collie-sized congregation in the cathedral-type building to the church that always has been served either by a minister fresh out of seminary or by one who is overdue for retirement.

The second most productive beginning point for those seeking to understand the middle-sized church is to examine the congregational culture, the theme of the first chapter.

Both of these characteristics can be understood more readily by examining in detail several distinctively different types of middle-sized churches. In each one the differences in culture stand out very clearly, but perhaps in no case can these differences be measured so precisely as in the contrast between those congregations that are accumulating capital and those that are living off accumulated capital.

Capital Formation or Capital Consumption?

Trinity Church is an eleven-year-old new mission that recently finished paying off the mortgage on its first unit. That first unit included six classrooms, restrooms, the pastor's office, a secretary's office with an adjoining workroom, and a multi-purpose room that could serve as the fellowship hall or seat 160 to 175 for corporate worship.

A year ago the congregation began planning for a permanent sanctuary and has secured two-year pledges in a building fund campaign that was concluded a few weeks ago. The leaders are hoping to begin construction within the next eight to twelve months and they all understand the necessity of at least one more, and probably two more, building fund programs in the years ahead.

Trinity Church became a financially self-supporting congregation during its third year. Numerical growth has not been as rapid as was anticipated. The initial plans called for construction of the permanent sanctuary during the seventh or eighth year. Yesterday's members, however, did not want to go into a second construction program until the mortgage from that first unit had been retired.

The average attendance at Sunday morning worship at Trinity passed the one-hundred mark five years ago and has been climbing by about five or six each year. Two years ago the average was 117, last year 122, this year attendance is averaging 128, and the expectation is it will pass 135 next year. Many members are convinced that soon after the new building is in use, attendance will zoom up to 175 or 200. Others are skeptical of this expression of "architectural evangelism" but both groups favor a building program.

*　　*　　*

Bethany is a 113-year-old congregation that meets in a building located two miles west of the central business district of a large city. The building was completed in 1907, remodeled in 1924, and expanded in 1953. It will seat 460 at worship and has twenty-four classrooms.

Bethany Church peaked in size in 1951 with an average attendance of 550 at Sunday morning worship at two services. It now averages 135 and operates on a budget of $185,000 a year. Slightly over $90,000 is received from member giving,

$40,000 is income from the endowment fund, $20,000 a year is appropriated from an unrestricted $60,000 bequest that Mrs. Bodendein left to Bethany a year ago, and $35,000 is the net income from rentals of church-owned real estate, including four non-profit groups that have their offices in the church building.

Recently a heated debate over church finances divided the congregation into four camps. One group insists that all of the income from rentals should be allocated solely to the maintenance of this beautiful gothic structure. A third-generation member of Bethany insists, "We're asking future generations to subsidize today's members by at least $40,000 to $50,000 a year. That's the amount of deferred maintenance we're accumulating by our present policy of using rental income to balance the operating budget. Someday, someone will have to pay for what we're not doing now in maintaining this fine old building."

A second group insists that expenditures be reduced to match member giving or member giving be increased to cover all of the current operating budget. A proponent of this point of view argues, "It's ridiculous for us to have two full-time ordained ministers on the staff. The only justification that anybody offers is that it would be a sign of defeat to cut back to only one minister here when once we had three. We don't need eight paid lead singers in the choir and we can't afford two people in the office. I know an old building takes a lot of care, but we should be able to get by with one custodian. If I had the authority to do it, I could slash the budget by $75,000 and no one would notice the difference in our program!"

The third group is led by a forty-year-old man who argues, "Previous generations of members bought and paid for this white elephant and I don't see any problem in letting them pay to feed it. There are at least two dozen old-timers here who have remembered Bethany in their wills. By the time Mrs. Bodendein's estate is used up, someone else will have died and left us another bequest. Any reasonable person can see that we don't need more than a fourth of the space we've inherited and it costs a small fortune every year to maintain this place. As long as the members give what one would expect a congregation this size to give, I don't see any problem in using money from the endowment fund, the unrestricted bequests and rentals to balance the budget."

The fourth group is the smallest and expresses the greatest frustration. A sixty-three-year-old woman articulated the feelings of this group in these words, "It's a shame for us to spend all that money on ourselves! For years I've urged that at least half of all the income from the endowment fund be allocated to missions and every unrestricted bequest go into the endowment fund rather than just be spent to balance the operating budget. I think it's a disgrace that we pay strangers to sing in our choir and have two pastors for this tiny handful of people, but we never pay our denominational benevolences in full! It's been at least ten years since we paid our full share of missions, but we continue to throw money away on the non-essentials like there was no tomorrow. We're asking yesterday's members to pay for a luxurious life for today's congregation and I believe that's wrong!"

* * *

Grace Church was organized in 1903 and peaked in size in 1959 with worship attendance running between 350 and 400 on Sunday morning. During the fifties a group of farsighted members persuaded the congregation to adopt five goals. The first was to acquire all the land in the block in what once was a single family-residential neighborhood. The second was to construct a ten-room educational wing with a large fellowship hall in the basement plus a suite of church offices on the first floor. This was designed so one section of it that includes the offices, restrooms, and two meeting rooms can be heated and cooled separately from the rest of what is a large physical plant.

The third goal was the razing of several houses for off-street parking and the construction of a twenty-apartment, income-producing building at the far end of the block. The fourth was the creation of the Grace Church Foundation to receive bequests, legacies, and other special gifts.

The fifth legacy from that decade of dynamic leaders was a clause in the articles of incorporation of the Foundation that none of the income from the Foundation be used to meet the operating expenses of the congregation. The Foundation can spend only the income from what is now over $3 million in investments and is restricted to *(a)* gifts for missions, denominational causes, and similar benevolences, *(b)* scholarships, and *(c)* matching the congregation dollar-for-dollar on any capital expenditures required to maintain the real estate.

Twelve years ago, when the mortgage on that apartment building was retired, the congregation created another non-profit corporation to take title to that structure and to operate it as housing for middle-income families. The first priority was for persons in financial need who had been members of Grace Church for at least ten years before moving into the building. While the intention was to limit it to housing for the elderly, that was not spelled out in precise terms. Today the residents of the apartment building include seven women who have been long-term members of Grace and have been divorced after at least fifteen years of marriage. The trend is clear that gradually the apartment building is becoming a home, not for elderly members as was anticipated a dozen years ago, but for single-parent families. No one at Grace is disturbed by that change.

Today Grace Church averages 145 at Sunday morning worship, the members pay all the costs of operating the congregation, including a full share of the denominational expenditures for missions. The staff includes a full-time thirty-three-year-old pastor who lives in one of the two houses left in this block, a church secretary, and a retired farmer and his wife who are paid on a part-time basis to serve as custodians of the church and who live on a rent-free basis in the other single-family house in the block. They take exceptionally good care of the property. The apartment building is managed and the property cared for by a couple who live in the building. The Foundation receives between $100,000 and $200,000 every year in bequests and memorials. It offers a four-year, full-tuition scholarship to any high school graduate from Grace Church or any high school graduate living within three blocks of the building who enrolls in a Christian college. It also offers three-quarter cost scholarships to any child from a member family or from the immediate neighborhood who wants to attend the denominational summer camp.

Three years ago when the denomination had a huge capital funds appeal for missions, the Foundation offered to match the giving of the members with four dollars for each one dollar contributed by a member *if the congregation exceeded the quota assigned it by the denomination.* A year ago the Foundation matched the congregation dollar-for-dollar in a $150,000 renovation program that included a new roof on both the buildings plus a new heating system and other improvements. The church owes $42,000 on a note for the money it borrowed to finance its share of that effort.

In describing this congregation the minister commented, "One-fourth of our Sunday morning attendance comes from this block, one-fourth from within three blocks of the building, and one-half from beyond four miles of the building. We have sixty off-street parking spaces and we use at least forty-five or fifty of them every Sunday."

*　　*　　*

These three middle-sized congregations are approximately the same size. They vary in age and they vary in terms of the neighborhood setting. One is a numerically growing congregation and two have experienced a substantial decline in numbers during the past three or four decades. If one thinks in terms of a congregational culture, however, the biggest differences may be in the distinction between capital formation and capital consumption.

Trinity, like thousands of other new missions, is a vigorous, growing, future-oriented, closely knit fellowship of pioneers who share a common commitment to the creation of a center for the worship and praise of God out on the ex-rural frontier. It also is a congregation that clearly is in the capital formation stage of its history.

Bethany is a long-established congregation that has accumulated a huge quantity of capital assets in real estate and an endowment fund of nearly a half million dollars. It is a numerically declining parish that today is seriously divided over how it should allocate these accumulated capital resources. While it engages in this divisive debate, today's congregation is being subsidized directly by yesterday's generation of members who have bequeathed a large quantity of capital assets to Bethany and indirectly by tomorrow's generation of members who will inherit from today's members a neglected physical plant.

Grace Church, like Bethany, has accumulated a very large quantity of capital assets, but unlike Bethany and like Trinity, it continues to be accumulating capital resources as the corpus of the endowment grows and the value of a well-maintained plant increases with the passage of time.

The big difference between Grace and Bethany is that most of the current income from the accumulated capital at Grace Church is directed to missions, scholarships, outreach, and to encourage the support of missions, a sense of self-reliance and a priority on the education of today's youth by today's members. At Bethany the current income from these capital assets is used to subsidize today's congregation.

Which of these three congregations do you believe is the healthiest and most vital? Which would you prefer to join? Is your congregation in a capital formation or in a capital consumption state of its history? Do you see any effect of this on the congregational culture, values, and priorities?

A strong biblical argument can be and occasionally is made that by definition a Christian church should not be accumulating capital resources (Matt. 6:19-21). The combination of a human being's natural attachment to place (the Old Testament is, in part, a story of this attachment to place) and governmental regulations on the design and construction of places for public assemblage makes it difficult for a congregation not to accumulate capital resources.[1]

American Protestantism also has accumulated a long, growing, and depressing series of case studies on how a large endowment fund can blight a congregation. Bethany Church represents that aspect of capital accumulation by a worshiping congregation.

There are several reasons why this issue of capital accumulation is a matter of real concern for a growing number of middle-sized congregations.

1. Perhaps the least publicized is the fact that the number of bequests left to Protestant churches in the United States has at least tripled since 1960 and more likely quadrupled. (This author has no data on Canadian trends on this subject.)

2. From this observer's experiences one of the most effective means of undercutting the health, vigor, vitality, unity, and sense of mission in a congregation is for that parish to drift into the habit of using bequests, endowment income, and similar financial resources to balance the operating budget. When today's members are subsidized by the dead, by investments from the past, and by a few benevolent families, it is easy to develop an irresponsible dependency stance. The continued dependence on financial subsidies can become a debilitating component of the congregational culture.

3. A very substantial number of today's churches are "balancing the budget" by deferring maintenance of the meeting place to another day. In effect, they are accepting a subsidy from yesterday's members in the form of the use of a paid-for piece of real estate, and also are asking for a subsidy

from tomorrow's members by neglecting the upkeep of that property.

4. Thousands of middle-sized congregations are meeting today in large, and sometimes functionally obsolete, buildings erected a few generations ago when labor costs were low and no one worried about energy conservation. This list includes a large number of black, Asian, and Hispanic churches meeting in used buildings purchased from Anglo congregations in the central city or one of the older suburbs.

5. A reasonable and justifiable distinction sometimes can be made between the operating budget of a congregation, including benevolences, and the expenditures required for major capital improvements such as a new heating system, the acquisition of land for off-street parking, or the purchase of a residence for the pastor. Experience suggests that while each generation of members should pay all operating costs, it does not impair the spiritual or psychological health of a parish when a portion of these capital costs is paid by a different generation of members than those who incurred the expenditure. The most common example is the ten- or fifteen-year mortgage for a new building. Those who planned the structure and made the decision to build it paid part of the cost and deferred part to be paid by members who have not yet joined. Grace Church represents another example. Today's capital expenditures are shared equally between today's members and some of yesteryear's members who left money to the Grace Church Foundation.

6. Despite all the criticisms leveled at them, religious bodies have earned an excellent record as good stewards. The churches, for example, have a far better record on the stewardship of land and buildings than American coal companies or the steel industry. That point frequently is overlooked.

7. One of the remarkable developments of the second half of this century has been the emergence of a growing number of older persons, mostly widowed women, but also some single,

never-married mature adults and many retired couples who have accumulated what to them is an amazing amount of wealth. These people have firsthand recollections of the Great Depression. They also are enjoying better health and a longer life expectancy than any previous generation of mature adults in history. Between 1970 and 1981 Americans age sixty-five and over experienced a more rapid increase in their income, and they accumulated wealth at a faster pace than any other age cohort. "Poor" and "elderly" or "widowed" and "poor" no longer are automatic synonyms.

8. The new church development surge of the fifties and the church construction boom of the fifties and sixties produced thousands of new houses of worship. Today these buildings no longer offer the maintenance-free subsidy that congregations enjoyed for a dozen or more years. The "twenty-year guarantee" has run out on what once was a new building. It now requires expensive care as well as an occasional renovation.

9. Finally, a great many congregations of all sizes have concluded they cannot afford to make the capital expenditures necessary to maintain, and perhaps expand, their property, and also to finance a full-scale program including outreach.

A growing number of churches have looked at these factors and concluded that a wise course would be to incorporate as a separate legal entity a local church foundation. (In some denominations this is not necessary since a denominational foundation will take care of all the legal and investment details, but will allow the local board to make all policy decisions.) This foundation receives bequests, memorials, and special gifts and administers their investment and use. The key factors in establishing such a separate body are *(a)* a separate set of trustees—a majority of whom do not hold any other policy-making office in that congregation while serving as trustees of the Foundation and not more than one person can serve both as a member of the governing board of the congregation and a trustee of the Foundation at the same time, *(b)* the development of an "arms' length" relationship between the congregation and the Foundation so the church does not become dependent on the Foundation for operating expenses, *(c)* the limiting of most grants to the congregation to matching grants for capital expenditures, expenditures for operation and maintenance of the property, funds for new ministries or programs (such as funding an aggressive evangelistic strategy), for missions and for scholarships, and *(d)* the reporting of the assets and expenditures of the Foundation be kept separate from the financial reporting system of the congregation.

In addition, the Foundation can offer a response to that growing number of older people who are living off a combination of current income and accumulated capital and who are concerned that "I don't want to outlive my money and be dependent on others." Understandably some of these people may feel severely limited in current giving, but they do want to give to their church. The church can help them in this dilemma by encouraging them to include the church in their will. The Foundation, which can be designated as the beneficiary for bequests and which also can acquire and hold title to real estate, can meet this need. Scores of churches have followed this procedure which can assure the donor that the stipulations will be followed, which removes temptation from the governing board of the congregation or finance committee to "borrow" from endowment funds, which also makes financial assistance available to the congregation for both capital needs and outreach ministries, and which can keep real estate worries off the congregational agenda and allow the leaders to concentrate on a ministry agenda.

As emphasized earlier, endowment funds controlled by the finance committee and policy makers tend to have a blighting impact on stewardship while foundations tend to have a creative and helpful impact. In many congregations the trustees of the Foundation are members who hold *only* that one position of responsibility for that period of time. This restriction reduces the temptation for the congregation to become heavily dependent on the Foundation. This restriction also opens the door to the use of the "matching grant" concept, whereby the trustees of the Foundation agree to use accumulated capital assets to match the giving of the members for inaugurating new ministries or for mission or for a new building program.

To implement such a program in most congregations often requires the creation of a committee of persons who make a commitment to visit a combined total of 100 members annually. At least four members of this committee should be individuals with a high level of competence in estate planning, tax legislation and accounting while another four or six should excel in interpersonal relationships and be respected and held in high esteem by longtime members of that parish. Their visits are designed to explain the purpose and value of the Foundation to potential benefactors and to describe alternative methods of contributing to the Foundation.

One other alternative also should be mentioned here, although the audience is more limited. This approach applies to those congregations which *(a)* have limited financial resources from the contributions of living members, *(b)* are located at a strategic site that the denominational officials have identified as critical for a Christian witness (near a community college that does not have a full-time campus pastor or across the street from the state capital or in a strategic inner city location), and *(c)* are served by a minister(s) who functions both as the pastor of that congregation and as a servant leader in that particular outreach ministry.

Some of these congregations operate with two budgets. One covers the costs of all aspects of congregational care, including regular corporate worship, the congregation's share of the total cost of maintaining that meeting place, and the benevolent giving by members. That budget is financed completely by member giving. The second budget covers all costs of that particular expression of Christian witness and

44

outreach, including a portion of the minister's compensation and part of the costs of maintaining the property. That budget is financed by denominational grants, income from rentals, proceeds from the endowment fund and memorials or some combination of those sources.

This system enables the congregation to see itself as a financially self-supporting ministry and yet enables that witness to be conducted without its being an excessive financial drain on the congregation.

As one reflects on the differences between those congregations that are accumulating capital and those that are living off the capital accumulated by past generations, one is struck by the contrast between a vigorous and optimistic future-orientation and a persistent and often pessimistic past-orientation. This strong past-orientation is also frequently a characteristic of the ex-neighborhood church.

Whatever Happened to the Neighborhood Church?

"My father was the first pastor of this congregation when it was founded in 1923," reminisced Herman Edwards, the son of the founding pastor and one of the five members of Lakeview Church who carry firsthand recollections of the congregation that predates World War II. "The farms out here on the west side of the city were being subdivided and scores of new homes were being built. At the time, old First Church downtown was far and away the biggest congregation of our denomination in the whole state. Earlier they had sponsored the Beechwood Church and a couple of others. In 1921 they purchased three residential lots on the corner and in the following year several of the men came out and organized a Sunday school.

"About that same time First Church hired a contractor, who was a member of that congregation, to build a house on one of those lots. At the time, my father was serving a church in a little county seat town about forty miles north of here and he was asked to come and be the first minister. We moved here in the summer of 1923. My mother was delighted with the move because we had indoor plumbing and electric lights in that new house. That was the first time in her whole life she had ever enjoyed those luxuries. I was ten years old at the time First Church sent about a dozen families out to be the nucleus and agreed to pay Dad's salary for the first year. He got $60 a month those first years, which was a $10 a month increase over what he had been paid where he had been before. Dad spent a lot of days, and most of the evenings, walking up and down the streets out here calling on the folks. Our church history reports that by 1938 we had over 200 members.

"Since I was the minister's son, it was expected I would get an education, so unlike most of the boys in this neighborhood, I stayed in school until I graduated from high school in 1931. That was a bad year and there simply wasn't any money for me to go on to college. I felt real lucky that Mr. Morrison, who was the leading member of our church, offered me a job in his hardware store over on Washington Avenue. I had to be there to open the store at seven o'clock in the morning. He paid me a dollar a day. That was a lot more than it may sound like to you today. The church had raised my father's salary to $75 a month in 1927, but by 1933 they had to cut it back to $35. My $26 or $27 a month was almost as much as his cash salary.

"By the time Martha and I were married in 1940 business had recovered to some extent," continued Mr. Edwards. "We were married in the church, of course. I remember it was raining that afternoon, but everyone who drove to our wedding could park within a block of the front door of the church. This was still a closely knit neighborhood and over on Washington Avenue, in addition to Mr. Morrison's hardware store were a couple of restaurants, a motion picture theater, a half dozen gas stations, a grocery store, and lots of other businesses, nearly all of them run by their owners.

"I had hurt my back when I fell off a ladder in the store, so I was 4F during the war. When Mr. Morrison died in 1943 I bought the business from his widow. Right after the war business really boomed for several years and at one point I had six people working full time for me. In the fifties, however, these strip shopping centers opened and offered off-street parking right in front of the stores. A dozen years later the big shopping malls came along and they just about wiped us out. By the time I decided to retire in 1978, Martha and I were running the store with the help of a high school student who came in after school every day to stock the shelves. I couldn't find a buyer, so we had a sale and I sold the building for what really was about the value of the land. I guess we were lucky to be able to stay in business as long as we did. The fellow who bought it opened a variety store and in two years he went broke. The bank now owns the building; it sits empty with about half of the other stores over on Washington Avenue. The movie theater closed twenty years ago and has been torn down to provide parking for a fast-food joint that is on the site of the old five and ten cent store.

"The year after we were married, we borrowed enough money from Martha's father to buy a house a block south of the church. We bought it from the original owner and when we moved in at least a third of the houses on that street were occupied by their original owners. A woman who is now a widow moved into a house at the other end of the block with her husband about 1940 or 1941, and today we're the only ones in that block who go back as far as 1960. At least half of the houses are rented, although in the past couple of years we've had several young couples come in and buy up one of those old houses and fix it up. To tell you the truth, however, I only know two of those couples personally. All of our friends have moved farther west or north, and none of them live within five miles of here. That includes all of our friends here in the church. Martha and I have talked about moving a few times, but I guess we never will. Her arthritis is pretty bad and my back keeps me from doing any lifting. That's the real reason why we closed the store. I just couldn't take it anymore standing up all day or even lifting the smaller boxes. Thirty-five years ago I reckon I could call by name at least a thousand people who lived in this neighborhood, and I could recognize the faces of at least a thousand more. That's because they came to the store, of course. Now, if I walked down every street around here, I doubt if I could call fifty by name, maybe not even thirty.

"Martha and I have four children. They're all married, but only one, our older daughter, lives in this state and she is over one hundred miles away. The kids don't hang around the old neighborhood like my generation did.

"When my father was the pastor of Lakeview Church," he continued, "there were four other mainline Protestant churches within three blocks of our building. We're the only one left. The Presbyterians sold their property to a Nazarene group in the early fifties and relocated to a big parcel of land four miles northwest of here. I hear they have over a thousand members. The Baptists had a big split several years ago and all of their best givers walked out with the crowd that started a new church. The group that remained was too small and too poor to make it and now their building is a funeral home. The Episcopalians got a priest who apparently was too liberal. The members scattered and the diocese sold the building to an independent Church of Christ group. The Lutherans had a fire about six years ago, I heard it was arson, that completely destroyed their church. They took the insurance money and relocated.

"As I told you, we're the only one left. Our church peaked in size in the early fifties. We can seat between 300 and 320 including the choir loft, and on at least half of the Sundays it would be full or nearly so. Gradually, however, as the neighborhood declined, our membership shrunk. Every time one of these other churches closed or moved away, a few of their people would come to Lakeview, but the only big influx was in the early sixties when First Church relocated from downtown to the far east side and we picked up thirty families who lived out this way. They came just in time to help us pay for the new educational wing we built in 1958 on the site of the old parsonage where I had lived for seventeen years. That kind of hurt to see our old home demolished, and I guess it was just as well neither of my parents were still around to see it happen. They put an awful lot into this church during the eighteen years my father was the minister here.

"The high school I attended has been closed and the building has been remodeled into the headquarters for the Board of Education," recalled Herman. "The elementary school I attended when we first moved here back in 1923 was torn down and replaced by a new building, but half the kids are bussed in so the PTA doesn't amount to much. For forty years my social life, my family life, my religious life, and my recreational life all took place in that space between where we lived and where I worked. Martha and I still go to church in this neighborhood, but everything else has changed. Our family is scattered among three states, our social life is spread across the west side of the city, we drive five miles to a shopping mall and three miles to buy groceries. Every winter we spend a couple of weeks in either Arizona or Hawaii. If we want to take in a movie, it's a five- or six-mile drive. Our very closest friends live four and seven miles from here.

"Today we run between 120 and 130 on Sunday morning," concluded Mr. Edwards, "which isn't bad I guess compared to a lot of other churches, but I doubt if there is even a dozen of us who walk. The rest drive and come from all over. Our Sunday school is down to maybe 35 or 40, but I guess that's natural considering most of us who are regulars are in the retirement years. The most helpful sign is our new minister. She came about two years ago and is the first woman minister we've ever had. She's the best preacher we've had since Mr. Harrison left nearly thirty years ago, and she's full of energy and ideas. She's got a youth group going, she reorganized the choir and got a new choir director and it's nearly double what it was. Before she came, we were down to about a hundred on

Sunday morning, but attendance really picked up after she came. She gets out and calls on people and that makes a big difference. A few of the folks were a little upset before she came when they heard she was divorced and had two teenagers, but that's really not a problem today. A lot of us now have a son or daughter who's been divorced so we're not as judgmental as we would have been thirty years ago. Two of our kids have been divorced and one is remarried. Martha and I were shocked and we really didn't like it, but you learn to adjust. If we can keep our minister for another five or six years, I believe our church may have a future."

The name of this congregation really is not Lakeview Church. It is legion. It represents a very large number of middle-sized congregations in urban or older suburban communities which no longer are really communities. Two sets of lessons can be gleaned from Herman Edwards' account. The first set can be described as diagnostic comments, and they can help us understand why the neighborhood or geographical parish has been following running boards, afternoon newspapers, the five- and ten-cent stores, and the one-room county schools into oblivion.

From a diagnostic perspective the world has changed. The day when people lived, worked, shopped, worshiped, played, socialized, and eventually retired in the same community has disappeared with the coming of the automobile, growing affluence, expanding choices, the sharp increase in entitlement programs for the middle class, the emergence of a national job market, and the disappearance of community based on geographical proximity.

The primary focal point for social interaction has moved from the neighborhood to the place of work. The decrease in the length of the work week has enabled most people to add several points of social interaction to their lives. In addition to the home and the place of work, these may include the country club or a health club, a cabin by the lake or a motorboat on the lake, a second job, the church, a vacation to Florida or Hawaii or the Rockies or the Smokies or Arizona, a nursing home or retirement center for some of the growing number of mature adults or night classes for adults or the tennis court or frequent visits with kinfolk several hundred miles away.

The distance between the place of work and the place of residence is increasing as is the distance between the place of residence and the place of medical treatment or between the place of residence and the place of worship.

Change has made the geographical parish an obsolete concept. Next Sunday thousands of Protestant ministers will drive past a church of their own denomination on their way to lead corporate worship with the congregations they serve.

For the congregation founded as a geographical parish this change usually produces seven choices.

1. Relocate to a new site "out where our kind of people now live."

2. Accept gradual decline and eventual dissolution.

3. Find a new minister with a magnetic personality to attract a new clientele. However the demand for these ministers greatly exceeds the supply.

4. Merge with a sister church in an effort to prolong the institutional life of both.

5. Attempt to reconstitute itself as a geographical parish around the current population of the neighborhood. This is exceptionally difficult because few of the current residents live or think in geographical terms or possess strong neighborhood loyalties. Most are simply passing through.

6. Redevelop the neighborhood as a place where the residents feel and express a sense of comradeship, community and mutual support. This was a popular approach back in the sixties and early seventies when community organization was perceived as the means for re-creating in older urban sections of the nation a new sense of community. It was expected that this would also provide the context for renewing or revitalizing neighborhood institutions, such as retail stores, libraries, physicians' offices, churches, parent-teacher asso-

ciations, scouting, and other voluntary associations. Too often, however, the value systems, the goals, the organizing techniques, and the priorities of those doing the organizing did not coincide with the cultural values and priorities of the new residents. Very few mainline denominational churches found this to be the path to creating a new role and a new future in the older residential neighborhoods of urban America. Few of the newcomers conceptualized their world in terms of a geographical expression of life.

7. Redefine the role as a non-geographical parish and inaugurate a specialized ministry to reach and serve a segment of the population whose needs are largely overlooked by existing churches in that part of the world. This specialty may range from organizing an early childhood development center with a weekday preschool program to developing a ministry with families that include a developmentally disabled member to creating a ministry with single parents to specializing in an outreach to and with those who share a strong interest in social justice.

When confronted with these choices, the leaders of the ex-neighborhood church often are reluctant to surrender the concept of the geographical parish. They may have difficulty choosing among the choices and frequently do not feel competent to identify and implement a new role. Rarely does it happen without the leadership of an aggressive, creative, and influential pastor who is willing and able to be an initiating leader.

One example of a highly specialized middle-sized congregation that serves a non-geographical clientele is the women's fellowship.

The Women's Fellowship

"The basic reason I joined this church was because of the very strong committee on Women and the Church here. A friend of mine at work told me about it, and after about six months of repeated invitations I finally gave in to her and came," explained Rosalyn Tresh, one of the newer members of Hillsdale Church. "The first thing that struck me was instead of the traditional clothbound hymnal in the pew racks, there were these paperbound songbooks. Every one of the sexist hymns either had been eliminated or rewritten. The second thing I noticed was the minister's reference to 'God our Mother and Father.' There were none of the usual sexist references anywhere in the service.

"I've been here nearly a year now, and as I look back on it, those things don't impress me as much today as they did on that first visit," she continued. "I guess there are three factors that have combined to make me such an active member in what is really a very short time. By far the most important is the Women's Book Circle. This was organized about eight months ago by our minister as an adult study group. We meet every Tuesday evening to discuss a book we're all supposed to be reading. We begin by sharing our personal concerns and frequently we never get around to discussing the book we're supposed to be reading. It's really a mutual support group. I'm fifty-three years old and four years ago my husband and I were divorced. We had been married for twenty-seven years and one day he came home and said he wanted to be free to go his own way alone. Six months later he was remarried, so I'm not so sure he wanted to go his own way alone. I think he wanted to go his own way without me. I hadn't worked since before our first child was born, so I had to go out and get a job and find a place to live. Our youngest child was in high school when this happened, and she lived with me for two years, but now she's gone off to college so I'm all alone. The Book Circle is my family.

"The second thing I like about this church is the minister. He's also been divorced so he has some idea of what that's all about, although he has remarried. He's a very kind, gentle, loving, understanding minister and he gives every one of us a big hug as he greets us when we leave after the service. While he's younger than some of us, he's the real father figure around here and some of us need that. I didn't know his first wife, but his new wife is a member of the Book Circle and one of my closest friends here. She was widowed a year after her first baby was born. Her second husband walked out on her and the three kids the day after her fortieth birthday, so she knows what it's all about.

"The third thing that keeps me here is the Committee on Women and the Church. I'm not as active with that group as I should be, but that committee has wiped out practically all traces of discrimination toward women in the congregation. This church is the only place I know where there is no blatant discrimination against women."

Rosalyn Tresh's story introduces us to another type of middle-sized church that has its own distinctive congregational culture. These congregations are still relatively rare, but their numbers are growing.

Hillsdale Church illustrates many of the characteristics of this type of congregation. It averages between 100 and 125 at Sunday morning worship, of whom 70 percent are women. Eight of the fifteen members on the church council are women, but three of the men rarely attend. It has a very strong and closely knit therapy group, which in this case carries the label, the Women's Book Circle. Seven of the eight members of the missions committee and all nine of the members of the Christian education committee are women. Four of the seven members of the finance committee, which is chaired by a bachelor, are men, but the most influential person on that committee is a woman who is a certified public accountant, has her own small firm, and is accused sometimes of running the committee.

The most dynamic group at Hillsdale is the Social Justice Committee and their top three priorities are nuclear disarmament, world hunger, and support of the day-care center housed in a church of another denomination one block down the street. Six of the nine members of that committee are women.

From the leaders' perspective the most troublesome aspect of life at Hillsdale is that the congregation limps along from one financial crisis to another. The bills always get paid, but rarely on time. The three biggest contributors would be considered as "only a little above average" if they were members at First Church downtown. The pastor, after nearly twenty-five years in the pastoral ministry, receives a stipend that is about two thousand dollars more than that of the typical seminary graduate in the first year of the first pastorate. A half dozen money-raising activities during the course of the year help finance programs and purchases that get squeezed out of the budget.

The Hillsdale congregation is a very closely knit and supportive fellowship. One divorced mother of three says, "When I was growing up, I went to church with my family. Now I come here to be with my family." That inner fellowship circle at Hillsdale includes two mothers who have never been married and never intend to marry, a widowed man with a face that was badly scarred in an accident, and a substantial number of individuals who have "come here to make a new start" and are well along the road to making a success of that new life. On the outer edge of that inner circle are a number of members who sometimes are referred to as "our wounded birds." These individuals, most of whom have serious psychological or physical handicaps, deeply appreciate this caring community and find their self-esteem gradually being strengthened by the redemptive spirit of this fellowship.

Five other characteristics of Hillsdale Church represent the distinctive personality of this specialized type of middle-sized congregation. First, the walls are alive with color, challenging posters, announcements of meetings and workshops in the larger community, pictures of members and decorations. The first-time visitor quickly gains the impression this congregation is alive and in motion, not resting on recollections of yesterday. Second, the Christian education committee is widely praised throughout the denomination in that region for its creativity, innovative programs, and openness to new ideas. Third, very few of today's leaders were in a leadership position in that congregation five years ago. Fourth, Sunday morning worship almost always has a strongly "upbeat" or positive ring to it.

The fifth distinctive characteristic is one that arouses ambivalent feelings when it is discussed. In recent years Hillsdale has seen a couple of dozen highly involved members leave and join other congregations, although the geographical distance from place of residence to church was clearly not the reason for the change. Well over one-half of these are persons who have remarried and gone off to make a new start with a new spouse in a new congregation.

Others are persons who came to Hillsdale while engaged in that struggle to make a fresh beginning in life. After they made that transition, they transferred their membership to another church. One of these ex-members reflected on her experience in these words. "I will always be deeply indebted to the people here at Hillsdale. They took me in and sheltered me when I badly needed that support. They loved me when no one else loved me. Now that I'm able to make it on my own, I decided it might be better to move on to a different church where the people would come to know me as I am, not as I was. Sometimes I feel guilty that I should be back at Hillsdale helping carry the burdens of others, but I'm not quite up to that yet. I have many close friends back there and I will never forget what those folks did for me, but I'm convinced the time has come for me to move on to a new chapter in my life."

When the subject of this exodus comes up, several of the members express feelings of resentment or of being rejected by these people whom they sometimes identify as "dropouts." The pastor is trying to encourage people to see these ex-members as "our graduates" who have gone off somewhere else to graduate school. How would you identify them?[2]

The number of congregations resembling Hillsdale Church is increasing. They rarely exceed 140 to 160 in attendance on Sunday morning, but it would be difficult to find a male-dominated counterpart to it. The closest may be the racially integrated church.

The Racially Integrated Church

"After thirty years of worshiping in racially integrated congregations on military posts, my wife and I naturally looked for a salt-and-pepper congregation after I retired," explained one of the black members of Greenwood Church. "We were a little surprised that we had to look so long and drive so far to find it, but we're glad we didn't give up until we found this church. Thanks to President Harry Truman, the armed forces were integrated while I was still in high school. Oh, I encountered a lot of prejudice, but it was all unofficial. Whenever I was stationed in this country, my wife was with me and we usually saw only three choices. We could go to a black church off post, we could be one of a handful of blacks in a predominantly white congregation, or we could worship with an integrated congregation on base. Since we believe very strongly in the racial integration of our society, we voted with our feet for what we believed in. We're trying to live out that tradition here in this congregation."

"My husband and I moved to this neighborhood back in 1955, right after he was discharged from the army," explained one of the white members. "This was an all-white neighborhood back in those days, and, of course, this was an all-white church.

"About fifteen years ago, when the neighborhood first began to change, there was some talk about whether or not we should relocate, but our new minister wouldn't even discuss it. While he is theologically very conservative, he was and is pretty liberal on the race issue. Most of our members moved away, and at one time we were down to about four or five dozen people on Sunday morning. For five years our minister had a part-time job, since we couldn't pay a full salary. Gradually, however, we began attracting a few of the new residents who are black and also quite a few younger white couples who are strong believers in racial integration. Only a few live around here, but they are real dependable. We're now averaging close to 135 at worship on Sunday morning, but our Sunday school is less than half that. My husband and I are staying, but sometimes we wonder what the future will bring. We still have the same minister, and he's real good at bringing in the whites who want to be part of a biracial church, but I don't know what will happen if this ever becomes a predominantly black church. For the past several years we have maintained a ratio of about 60 percent white and 40 percent black."

"I'll tell you what will happen if the blacks become a majority here," declared a black woman in her fifties. "The whites will leave! Not all of them, of course, and I know you wouldn't leave, Honey," she added as she nodded in the direction of the other lady, "but most of them would leave. The only way to have a racially integrated church is for the whites to be a clear majority. If I had wanted to be in a black church, I would have joined one. There are plenty of black churches within walking distance of my house. I chose to be part of a congregation that includes both blacks and whites. That's why I came here and I want to keep it this way!"

"This is a wonderful congregation and I can't think of anywhere else I would rather serve," observed the minister at a subsequent meeting with a visitor. "I came here before blacks began to move into this neighborhood and I believe that is very important. I've been here sixteen years now and all of the black members plus four-fifths of the whites have joined since I came. If you'll pardon my lack of humility, I'm the central thread in the continuity here. The continuity is not in the building, except for a few of our longtime white members, it's not in the denominational affiliation, or in the program. The three threads of the continuity are the desire of the members to be part of an interracial fellowship, our conviction that God has called each of us to carry out this witness, and me.

"I don't want to minimize the importance of our leaders, both black and white, but we've had three almost complete turnovers in the lay leadership since I came. Today our five most valuable leaders are: (1) a black elementary school principal who joined only three years ago, (2) a retired black colonel from the Air Force, (3) a retired white banker, (4) a white social worker in her early fifties, and (5) a young childless couple who drive sixteen miles each way to be a part of our congregation. The banker is the only one who was a member here six years ago."

These comments introduce another distinctive type of middle-sized church. One of the reasons they tend to be middle-sized, rather than large, is the problem of stereotypes. The typical racially integrated church in which at least 30 percent of the members are black and at least another 30 percent are white is small enough that every member can know every other by name. That largely eliminates the temptation to think in stereotypes about "honkies" or "niggers."

This is one of several of the distinctive characteristics of the racially integrated church. It is large enough to justify a full-time minister who often is a central thread in the continuity, but small enough for the members to know one another as persons.

Perhaps the most critical characteristic is hope. Several years ago, in a study conducted for the Johnson Publishing Company, Daniel Yankelovich reported that the basic division splitting the black population of the United States down the middle was the distinction between hope and hopelessness. One-half of the blacks despair of any bright future for them within the present system. The other half of the black population expressed at least moderate faith in the American system and were convinced it is possible to achieve equality within that system. The predominantly white racially integrated church draws its black members from among those who share this hope.

The second most critical factor in creating and maintaining a racially inclusive church, and some will argue this is the number one variable,[3] is a pastor who is committed to that goal, who loves people, who is willing and able to spend considerable time as a warmhearted pastor with the older white members, who is convinced it can happen, who is willing to lead, who believes in the value of long pastorates, and who also is a very patient human being.

The typical predominantly white, but racially integrated, church also shares many of the following characteristics: (1) it is a non-geographical parish, (2) adults usually outnumber children by a very large margin, (3) several of the most influential leaders are hard-working black women who are determined to make this venture a lasting success, (4) a disproportionately large number of the adult males served in the armed forces and were part of a racially integrated congregation while in military service, (5) on Sunday morning the congregation is between two-thirds and three-quarters female, (6) every black visitor receives a warm welcome and a follow-up visit, (7) fellowship is more important than adult classes in the program, (8) the congregation rarely encounters the freedom of no financial worries, (9) social workers and educators constitute a large proportion of the leaders, (10) an above average proportion of the members are active leaders in the regional judicatory of that denomination, (11) there is widespread agreement that the future of this role depends on continuing as a predominantly white congregation and therefore both black and white members always rejoice when the next class of new members is predominantly white, (12) the children's division of the Sunday school may be the only place in which blacks constitute a majority, and (13) rarely is the meeting place of the racially integrated church located in a neighborhood where there is a widespread fear of violent crime at night.

In several respects the racially integrated church has more in common with the women's fellowship than with nationality congregations, but all three tend to rank at the low end of the middle-sized range when churches are categorized by size.

The Urbanization of the Nationality Parish

"We're a tiny minority within the Lutheran Church—Missouri Synod," explained the pastor of the 320-member Concordia Church. "Most people see our denomination as German, but we have only one parish left that is strictly a German-language church. Few people realize we have more black parishes in the Synod today than German-language churches. The last time I looked in the yearbook there were only 73 congregations that offered a German-language service every Sunday, but we have at least 233 all-black or predominantly black parishes.

"At Concordia about 50 to 60 people come to the 8:30 German service on Sunday morning and we have close to 100 at the eleven o'clock English service. About a half-dozen graduate students at the University, who are Lutherans, attend the German service. One is from Germany, three are lifelong Lutherans who are getting ready to pass the German exam and want to combine worship with practice in German, and one is a teaching assistant in the German department.

"About half of the rest are in their seventies and older and are members who are more comfortable in German than in English. The rest are people, mostly in the thirty-five- to fifty-age bracket, who were born in Germany and have migrated to America. One younger couple, who came over about six years ago, never miss, and they always bring their three children with them.

"Twice I've turned down calls to more attractive parishes because the folks here were afraid they might not be able to find another minister who is bilingual," continued the pastor, "and I don't want to leave them in a lurch, but I really don't see a very bright future here. Forty years ago Concordia had 800 members and averaged over 600 on Sunday morning. What do you see ahead for us?"

While it is impossible to offer here a detailed prescription for Concordia, several comments can be made. First, this is a distinctive type of congregation. Scores of these parishes can be found in those denominational families that have not yet completed the process of being Americanized. The Baptist General Conference, the Evangelical Covenant Church, the Lutheran Church—Missouri Synod, the North American Baptist Conference, the Estonian Evangelical Lutheran Church (Ontario, Canada), and the Mennonite Church include many congregations that are still in the transitional stages. Far more numerous are the thousands of recently established congregations that have been organized since 1945 to serve people from the new immigration from the Pacific rim (especially Korea), Latin America, Cuba, and Puerto Rico.

Second, for the congregations in this category serving the immigrants from Europe and their descendants, the boats have stopped coming over. In 1892, 119,168 immigrants came to the United States from Germany and Austria and 66,295 from Scandinavia. Forty years later those figures were 2,670 and 938 respectively. Twenty-five years later, in 1957, the numbers had climbed back up to 6,189 immigrants from Scandinavia and 60,383 from Germany, but by 1982 were back down to 1,800 from Scandinavia and 6,700 from Germany while the number from Mexico was perhaps a million or more annually (although many of these returned to Mexico).

In other words, the growth in the number of nationality and language congregations is in those serving the Hispanic and Asian immigration.

Third, for those congregations that were established generations ago to serve the immigrants from Europe, the list of alternative courses of action is both short and challenging. Most of them will end up choosing from these six alternatives.

1. Complete that role as a nationality church and close with

a celebration of the fulfillment and completion of that role.

2. Plan for the day when the title to the real estate will be transferred to the denomination and denominational leaders will be asked to determine whether or not a new ministry to a new clientele should be launched from this place.

3. Intentionally and systematically plan to be two congregations under the same roof and probably financed out of the same budget. One congregation will be composed of those persons who want to be part of that nationality parish. The other congregation will be the members of what in effect would be a new mission that is meeting in this building that was constructed and maintained by the nationality congregation. This alternative requires *(a)* a minister who is competent and comfortable in both roles—as the part-time pastor of the nationality congregation and as the part-time mission developer of the new congregation, *(b)* a nucleus of 50 to 100 persons for that new mission, none of whom have had any previous affiliation with that congregation and none of whom are related by either blood or marriage to members of the nationality parish—this has to be a *new* start, *not an Americanized clone of the old, (c)* active and positive support for this concept by members of the nationality congregation and this includes paying a full-time salary for what they will perceive as part-time pastoral services and affirming the idea that strangers will benefit from the rent-free use of *our* building, *(d)* no overlap in program or schedule for the two congregations until after the new mission is at least as large as the nationality parish, and *(e)* a positive and hopeful view of the future.

4. Use the capital resources accumulated over the decades as a nationality parish to relocate to a new site and construct a new meeting house for a new congregation in a new era. This alternative was widely used in the 1945–60 era, often but not always with great success, but is more difficult today because of the lack of an obvious and widely agreed upon place to relocate and the much higher costs of land and construction.

5. Wait for a new wave of immigrants from "the old country" to come in and revitalize that congregation.

6. Consider the "third generation" phenomenon. Frequently, but not always, when the grandchildren of the original immigrants become adults, they seek to learn and affirm the culture and language their own parents renounced in the process of becoming Americans. This has turned out to be more attractive to Japanese-American congregations than to the German-American parishes and obviously will not work everywhere.

The primary purpose of including this chapter was to illustrate the huge diversity among what can be identified as middle-sized churches. The secondary purpose was to identify some of the distinctive characteristics of each type and to offer a few suggestions on alternative courses of action. The story of the middle-sized church would not be complete, however, without recognizing some of the key personalities who serve as lay leaders in the typical middle-sized congregation.

CHAPTER THREE

Six Key Personalities

The typical small membership church often resembles a family and the decision-making processes tend to resemble those found in families. Budgets usually are perceived either as an unnecessary luxury or a required task, but expenditures are influenced far more by income than by a predetermined budget figure. Many of the most far-reaching decisions are made at an ad hoc gathering of several members of the family. Kinship ties are far more influential than official titles or positions of authority. Sometimes one family literally does control that congregation.

By contrast, most of today's large congregations resemble a corporation more than a family. Power tends to be in the hands of those who have the authority of a particular office. The paid staff (or civil service) usually exercises more control than any one family. The "business of the church" is transacted at official meetings of the central governing board or by well-organized committees. The budget is an instrument of considerable influence and usually reflects a carefully thought-out set of priorities. To amend the budget means changing that set of priorities.

Between those two extremes is the middle-sized congregation. It is too large, too complex, and frequently the turnover in the membership is too rapid for it to function like a large family. On the other hand, the middle-sized congregation is too small for the members to accept the idea it should function as a large and complex bureaucracy. The sense of intimacy and the possibility of every member knowing every other member by name, and frequently as a friend or neighbor, means that trust tends to be placed in individuals, rather than in committees or boards or in a particular family. This is a central component of the congregational culture of the typical middle-sized church.

"If the Nelson family is in favor of that idea, I guess I can go along with it," agrees the person in the 65-member congregation. "If Roger Jones proposed it, I'll support it," declares the member of the middle-sized church. "If the finance committee has studied it and that's their recommendation, I don't see any reason why I should object," observes the member in the large church. As the size of a congregation increases, the focal point of trust shifts from a family to individuals to the organizational structure. The frequent lag in that sequence usually reflects the fact that most members perceive their church to be smaller than it really is.

In seeking to understand the role of personalities as a part of the culture of the middle-sized church, it may be useful to discard ecclesiastical terminology and turn for a moment to an anthropological frame of reference. The early social organization of Israel consisted of four subdivisions: families, clans (a clan consisted of a group of households or an extended family with common ancestry), tribes, and nations (Josh. 7:16-18). One contemporary parallel in American Protestantism can be seen in the way the very small congregations often resemble the family. Another parallel can be seen in those congregations averaging perhaps 65 to 100 at Sunday morning worship that often have at the center several households, many of which have a common ancestry, and thus resemble the clan. The contemporary counterpart to the tribe is the middle-sized congregation which may include several clans plus a number of families not related to any of those clans while the very large churches resemble the nation.

The ancient tribes were ruled by a council of elders that

usually consisted of the heads of the several families and/or clans (Gen. 36:15; Exod. 34:31). This system of governance still is followed in several denominations in which the council of elders constitutes the governing body for that congregation. Today, however, the qualifications for becoming an elder often are commitment and competence rather than age and kinship ties, but that is far from a universal generalization!

While the head of the household often controls the family, a different organizational pattern exists in the tribe in which several individuals share influence while in the typical nation a few tribes (finance committee, board of trustees, Christian education committee, session or consistory, staff) possess a disproportionately large degree of influence.

Thus the identification of the key family or families is critical to an understanding of the internal dynamics of the small church, but in the middle-sized congregation certain personalities stand out, often without regard to family background. It may be useful to identify several of these personalities who are so influential in the life of the typical middle-sized congregation. The person to begin with, of course, is the most influential.

Uncle Harold the Patriarch

The new minister had been installed as the eleventh pastor of the sixty-nine-year-old Lake Avenue Church the previous September. The church had peaked in size during the mid-fifties when Sunday morning attendance averaged between 260 and 300. During the sixties most of the remaining "old families" moved farther west and the community now included a far larger proportion of single adults, young childless couples, Asians, widowed individuals, and ex-rural residents who had come to the city to find a job.

The previous pastor had experienced an unhappy three years and suddenly left with less than a week's notice to the congregation. The new minister had arrived to find a demoralized congregation averaging fewer than 100 at worship.

Seven months later the Sunday school had doubled from fewer than 30 children to nearly 50, worship attendance was running between 125 and 140, the interior of the building had been painted by a crew of volunteers, and morale clearly was up.

Given these changes, the new minister felt optimistic as this April Board meeting began and as he presented four proposals to the assembled crowd of nearly thirty leaders. Among those present was Harold Cole, the seventy-seven-year-old patriarch. Harold's father had been one of the key leaders in the organizing of this congregation back when it was seen as a new mission on "the far west side" of town. For more than forty years his son, Harold, had been one of the most active, loyal, and influential leaders in the Lake Avenue Church. Nine years ago, following a serious heart operation, Harold resigned from all leadership posts. Since his recovery he was always in church, but rarely attended any committee meetings.

While no one questioned his right to be present at this Board meeting, a couple of the members greeted his arrival with surprise. "It's such a beautiful evening I thought I'd just walk over and see how you're treating our new minister," explained Harold.

The new minister's first proposal was to offer an early service on Sunday mornig for the benefit of those who found it inconvenient to attend the eleven o'clock service. He was surprised by the negative response that this would "split the congregation into groups who would never see each other," overwork the organist, and complicate family schedules if the youth sang at that first service.

The new minister's second proposal was to remodel the pulpit-centered chancel to provide greater visibility for the communion table, move the pulpit to one side, balance that with a lectern on the other side, and move the choir to the balcony where they could reinforce the congregational singing. This was greeted with strong protests that people wanted to be able to see the choir, that some of the older choir members might not be able to climb the stairs to the balcony, and that the choir director might be offended to be demoted to the balcony. Even when the minister explained that the newly organized youth choir said they preferred to be in the balcony, it did not seem to change many minds.

The third proposal, to conduct a special financial campaign for support of the new denominational effort to raise more money for missions evoked a heated discussion on whether a church could afford to have two financial drives only five months apart without offending people and on whether this would reduce support for the local expense budget.

By this time the new minister's optimism was largely eroded, but he plunged ahead with a suggestion that the church begin now to plan for the opening of a weekday Early Childhood Development Center in September of the following year. The first response was to question whether this congregation should intrude on what really is the responsibility of the parents and the public schools. The second member to speak questioned the financial viability of the idea. A third raised doubts about securing competent staff for such a venture. The fourth response questioned whether or not the wear and tear on that twenty-nine-year-old educational wing might not be excessive in such a venture with three- and four-year-olds.

The new minister, who had discussed each of his four proposals with several of those present, felt betrayed, crushed, defeated, frustrated, and bewildered. For lack of a more attractive alternative, he turned to Harold Cole, who had remained completely silent during this discussion that had consumed nearly ninety minutes, and inquired, "Mr. Cole, you haven't said a word tonight; do you think any one of these ideas has any merit?"

After several seconds of silent reflection, Uncle Harold

responded, "Young man, as long as you preach the gospel and bring in the people, this congregation will support any changes you're convinced will make us a better church."

Ten minutes later, without another word from Harold Cole, the Board unanimously approved each of the new minister's four proposals.

*   *   *

"Before you make any proposals to the Board about changing the Sunday morning schedule for the summer, you better check with Harold Buck," suggested a longtime member to the new minister who had arrived the previous fall to become the forty-third pastor in the 137-year history of the Barton Ridge Church.

"Why should I check with him?" inquired the new minister. "He's no longer on the Board and he doesn't hold any other official leadership position in this church. If I check with him, that means I should talk to each of the other 273 members here. That would take all summer! In all fairness, if I go see Uncle Harold, I should spend an equal amount of time checking every proposal out with every other member. Why should I pay special attention to Uncle Harold?"

"I'll give you a half dozen reasons why you should check this out with Uncle Harold, as well as any other proposals you may have for changes around here," replied the longtime member who had become very fond of the new minister and who also was one of the "pillars" of the Barton Ridge Church.

"First, while Uncle Harold hasn't been on the Board officially for at least seven or eight years, through kinfolk and friends he can influence twelve to fifteen votes out of the twenty-four on the Board. Second, Uncle Harold doesn't like to be ignored. Third, Uncle Harold didn't get to be the most influential member of this congregation by losing. Fourth, I happen to know Uncle Harold likes you. He believes you're the best pulpiteer this congregation has had since the Reverend MacDonald was here forty years ago. But Uncle

Harold also believes you're a little pushy and you always want to have things your own way. He just might veto this one in the hopes of teaching you a lesson. Fifth, if you go to Uncle Harold and ask his advice, I expect he'll support your idea. If I've heard him say it once, I've heard him say a dozen times that we ought to move the schedule up an hour in the summer. If you've noticed, Uncle Harold doesn't like the heat. He perspires rather profusely in the summer. If you go to see him in the next day or two, by the time the Board meets next Tuesday evening, you'll have a majority in favor of the change even before you bring it up. Sixth, you're too young to be committing suicide, and ignoring Uncle Harold is one way to kill any future you have here as our minister."

"That's out and out manipulation," protested the pastor. "What you're suggesting is that I get involved in church politics. I've never liked that game and I'm not about to start now!"

"Take your choice," replied the old-timer quietly. "Do you want to manipulate the situation in a way that your proposal will be defeated because you ignored Uncle Harold? Or do you want to manipulate it in a way that your recommendation will get a fair and maybe a receptive hearing, by checking it out with Uncle Harold in advance? Either way, you're going to influence the response of the folks who will be at the Board meeting next week. There's no neutral course of action. I wouldn't be surprised if, after you introduce your plan for the summer schedule, someone on the Board may ask if anyone knows how Uncle Harold feels about it. Take your choice, my friend, do you influence the decision by checking this out in advance with Uncle Harold or by ignoring him?"

These encounters with the patriarch introduce two important considerations in the decision-making process of the middle-sized congregation. First, they illustrate a very basic ethical question. Are there value-free or neutral approaches to innovation? Or does every course of action carry a built-in bias? This is not the place for an extended discussion of that issue, but it is a very basic question. It is the position of this writer that value-free approaches do not exist. There are no neutral questions, procedures, processes, policies, or systems of congregational decision-making. Every one has a bias. The ethical question is to choose an approach that is consistent with one's values and goals.

Second, this conversation introduces the first of a few of the key personalities who help make each worshiping congregation different from all other churches.

Every church has an Uncle Harold. The distinctive characteristic of Uncle Harold is that no changes are made and no new ideas are implemented over his opposition. Uncle Harold did not get to be Uncle Harold by losing!

On some issues Uncle Harold may pass. He understands that it is better to express no opinion than to lose.

Uncle Harold's role also illustrates the difference between authority, the right to make or influence final decisions that is the product of an official position or office, and power, the influence that is a product not of official position, but of personality, good bloodlines, knowledge, charisma, politics, wealth, wisdom, tribal deference patterns, and/or age. Uncle Harold is a powerful figure, but often does not hold an official position of leadership. Uncle Harold is influential, but not always highly visible. In many congregations Uncle Harold sits in the same place in the same pew every Sunday while in other churches Uncle Harold only rarely attends public worship.

Uncle Harold may be a man or a woman and sometimes may be a family or a clan. The larger the number of members and organizations, the greater the probability there will be several Uncle Harolds in that congregation. One may have great influence over the property, another over finances, a third in the women's organization, a fourth in the choir, and a fifth in the Sunday school.

Sometimes Uncle Harold is a relatively passive patriarch or matriarch, occasionally Uncle Harold is the central leader in an effort to introduce changes or to expand the evangelistic outreach of that congregation or to allocate more money to missions or to enlarge the Sunday school. Typically, however, Uncle Harold has a greater attachment to the past than to the future, to the status quo than to change, and to the building than to outreach.

There are several other attributes to Uncle Harold that should not be overlooked. From Uncle Harold's perspective he is both a committed Christian and a loyal member of this congregation. Occasionally Uncle Harold may wonder why the Lord placed on him the burden of the general oversight of this congregation and the responsibility to keep it headed in the proper direction, but as a dedicated Christian Uncle Harold accepts this burden that the Lord has placed on his shoulders. Sometimes Uncle Harold wonders why this burden has been increased by the weight of the coming of the new minister, but what the Lord wills, the Lord wills.

In the small membership congregation Uncle Harold often is the patriarch of the central family in that church. In the very large congregation the senior minister often assumes Uncle Harold's role after having attained the necessary number of years of seniority.

In the middle-sized congregation Uncle Harold usually is one of the half dozen individuals who exert a profound influence on the values, priorities, role, and direction of that tribe. Who is the Uncle Harold in your congregation?

Katherine, the Keeper of the Tribal Legends

"We tried something like that here about eighteen years ago, it was in the Reverend Butler's second year as our minister, to be exact, but it didn't work then, so I don't see any reason why it would work today," declared Katherine Barkley, a veteran member of Trinity Church after hearing a report from the Christian education committee recommending creation of a Wednesday afterschool program for children in grades one through six. "We had nearly forty children in that age group at the time and only nine showed up, so we abandoned it after a month or so. Today our congregation is older and we have fewer than thirty children in that age group, so I don't see any reason why we should try it again."

"But our concern today is as much to reach children from unchurched families as to serve our own," protested the representative from the committee that had prepared the report. "I think we should at least give it a try."

"It may be a good idea," replied Katherine, "but history proves it won't work here."

After a long and very awkward silence, the person chairing the board said, "It is getting late and we have four other items of business we must discuss yet tonight. Maybe we can come back to your recommendation at another meeting." That recommendation for an afterschool program was never again discussed at Trinity Church.

*   *   *

"About five years ago we tried to raise some extra money for missions by a special appeal and we received more flak than money. Our people simply don't like special appeals," responded Henry Moore, the representative from the finance committee, to a request that a special offering be taken in response to a denominational appeal. "Here at Central Church we've operated with a unified budget for a good many years and I don't think we should impose any special appeals on our members."

"What we tried five years ago bears practically no resemblance to this proposal," declared Katherine Bauer, a longtime leader at Central Church. "That appeal was one individual's idea. This one comes to us from our denominational leaders. They have examined it and have given it their unreserved approval. Back in 1968 there was a special denominational appeal for missions and we supported it. In fact, this congregation gave 107 percent of our goal. We did it again about nine years ago when there was another denominational appeal and we raised nearly $4,600 against a goal of $4,000. It seems to me that our precedents all are consistent with this proposal and I don't see anything wrong with it."

Within seventy seconds a motion was made to approve and support the special appeal; it was seconded and adopted without a dissenting vote.

These two incidents illustrate another key personality in many middle-sized congregations. This is the keeper of the tribal legends, here identified simply as Katherine. This individual is the depository for all of the legends, traditions, rules, precedents, facts, statistics, and customs of that tribe. When the keeper of the tribal legends speaks, that is the voice of authority. Several years ago someone challenged the accuracy of a statement made by this keeper and was proved to be completely wrong; that was the last challenge from anyone. Even Uncle Harold usually will check his facts with the keeper of the tribal legends before speaking about precedents or traditions.

These individuals tend to come in one of two categories. Some, such as the keeper of the tribal legends at Trinity Church, are especially proficient at identifying precedents that will block any new idea. Others, and these are greatly appreciated by most pastors, resemble the veteran leader at Central Church. They possess a remarkable and persuasive ability to explain how there are no traditions or customs or precedents that can be used to undermine this new proposal to expand the ministry of the middle-sized church.

Here again the size of the congregation becomes a discernible factor. In the small church the influence of the keeper of the tribal legends may not be diminished by the fact that he or she does not currently serve on the governing board. In the middle-sized church this person almost always holds an official position while in the huge churches the keeper of the tribal legends often is a longtime staff member.

Dependable Dennis

"I have a problem," confided the pastor of St. Mark's Church to his closest friend in the congregation, Dennis Greer. "My wife simply does not like living next door to the church. People are forever walking in unexpectedly and we simply do not have any privacy. We've been here three years now and everything else is fine. I can see us spending the next seven to twelve years here, but only if we can get out of that ancient parsonage. In addition to the lack of privacy, it's an old building and we're forever having problems with the plumbing and electrical systems. It also really is too small. Our bedroom is the only one on the first floor. Pretty soon we'll be moving the baby to one of those three upstairs bedrooms. That means if she wakes up in the night, we may not hear her. Both of our boys like having their own room, but all three of those upstairs bedrooms are pretty small. My wife and I could move upstairs and move our oldest downstairs, but none of those upstairs bedrooms is large enough for a double bed."

A few weeks later at the monthly Board meeting Dennis asked for the floor. "Some of us have been talking about our future here as a congregation on the near west side. When this church was founded back in 1903, it was a neighborhood church. That's changed. If I'm not mistaken, only one of the members of this Board walked here tonight. Mary caught me just as our meeting began tonight and asked if I would walk her to her car when we're through tonight. She had to park two blocks down the street and she would rather not walk alone that far after dark. I wouldn't want my wife walking around this neighborhood alone at night.

"As I said, some of us have been talking and we're ready to suggest a four-part plan. The heart of it is we go out of the housing business. If we would tear down that old parsonage we could pave that whole lot and have between thirty and thirty-five parking spaces. That would take care of most of our evening meetings. Sundays are not a problem. There is plenty of street parking for the size of our crowd, but we need off-street parking for evenings and for special occasions like weddings and funerals."

"Where do you propose our minister would live?" inquired another member of the Board.

"That's the second part of our plan," replied Dennis. "We've checked around and nearly half of the pastors on this side of town already get a housing allowance. As I suggested a minute ago, let's get out of the housing business and into the parking business."

"How will we pay for this?" asked another person.

"That's the third part of our proposal," explained Dennis. "We should be able to raise $50,000 in a six-month financial campaign. That would pay for razing the old parsonage, grading, and paving the parking lot and leave maybe $10,000 that we could loan our minister for a down payment on a home they would own. I believe everyone here is very happy with our present minister and his wife, and I've been told that ministers who own their own home tend to stay longer than ministers who live in church-owned housing. That's the fourth part of this proposal, an effort to make sure we keep our minister for at least another six or seven years."

*   *   *

"Take a look at this one, Dennis, and tell me what you think," said the pastor of Bethany Church to a very close friend and confidant. The object of the conversation was an anonymous note criticizing the minister for "those simple-minded children's sermons that detract from our sense of worship every Sunday morning."

"That's the third negative comment I've had about my children's sermons in less than a month," continued Rev. Kim Wellington. "I've about decided to drop the children's sermon, at least for a while. What do you think?"

"Let me check around before you make up your mind," responded Dennis. "Don't make any changes until I've had time to check it out."

Ten days later Dennis reported back to the minister. "From what I've been hearing around, there are only two or three people who don't like your children's sermons. My hunch is that one of the two who complained to you personally also sent that anonymous note. There are at least forty or fifty families here with young children who think your children's sermons are more valuable than the Sunday school plus another three or four dozen adults who don't have children who say they really appreciate those simple and interesting messages. Don't let a couple of highly vocal people scare you."

"Thanks, Dennis," replied the minister. "It's awfully easy to let a couple of people spook you into believing they speak for the entire membership."

*   *   *

"You're right, Dennis, that was a pulpit committee here last Sunday," responded the fifty-six-year-old minister at Garrison Street Church to his closest friend and confidant. "While I did not give them any encouragement when we talked Sunday afternoon, I received a telephone call this morning from one of the members stating they were scheduled to meet tonight and that I should be available for a phone call tomorrow morning. What do you think I should tell them if they call?"

"Tell them you'll accept the call," replied Dennis.

"What! You're suggesting I leave here? While I try to keep myself open to the call of the Lord, I had pretty well made up my mind I would stay here until I retired," declared the obviously startled minister. "What are you trying to tell me, Dennis?"

"You asked for my opinion and you got it," replied Dennis. "Let's look at the facts. You're fifty-six years old, it's somewhat unlikely you will receive very many attractive calls as you get closer to sixty. You've been here for nearly fourteen years now, your kids have left home so you're free to move and you're in good health. If you want an honest opinion, I think you're ready for a new challenge. You're beginning to be a little complacent and some folks here are beginning to think the church is ready for a change. You always said you wanted to move a year too soon rather than stay a year too long. This call may be the word from the Lord that the time has come for you to move on to one more pastorate before you retire."

"I appreciate your candor," replied the minister, "but I never expected my best friend to tell me to move."

"I am your best friend," declared Dennis, "that's why I have to be honest with you."

Many ministers face three extremely sensitive problems because of the nature of their calling. One is to voice a legitimate personal concern that does not sound as if they are asking for favors or special treatment. If that parsonage was acceptable to the past fourteen ministers, it should be acceptable to the present pastor. The second is the temptation to take literally the admission, "There are a lot of us who feel the same way I do, but they're afraid to say anything." Or the anonymous notes that turn up on a pastor's desk. How widespread is that discontent? The third is perhaps the most complex of all. When is it time to move on to another place? Fortunate is the pastor who has a Dependable Dennis to turn to for counsel and help on those and similar issues.

Why Don't You Call Carolyn?

"John Boonstra died last night and the family would like to have some refreshments here at the church after they come back from the graveside services," explained a member of Calvin Church to the church secretary over the telephone one Tuesday afternoon.

"Why don't you call Carolyn?" came the response. "I think she's the one you want to talk to about that."

*   *   *

"The District Committee on Christian Education has scheduled a workshop to be held here at Wesley Church, and they want a couple of people from our congregation to help with the registrations as people come in that morning," reported one member to the minister.

"Why don't you call Carolyn?" replied the minister. "I think she'll be glad to help, and if she can't, she'll help you find someone who will."

*   *   *

"Mrs. Nettles has to go into the city to see a specialist for her diabetes every other Tuesday for the next two or three months," explained a member to the rest of the Board at Calvary Church. "She lives alone, she doesn't drive, and she doesn't have any relatives here. Can any of you suggest someone who could drive her into the city?"

"Why don't you call Carolyn?" suggested one Board member. "She doesn't work, she has a car, and she probably would be glad to do it."

*   *   *

"The trustees have agreed to partition off that corner at the end of the corridor for a Sunday school supply room and to build several shelves along three walls. They have promised to have it completed by the end of the month," reported the chairperson of the Christian education committee at St. Paul's Church to the other members of the committee. "Now we need someone who will gather up all the supplies, sort them out, and arrange them on the shelves. Anyone here want to volunteer for that job?"

After a long and embarrassing silence, one of the committee members offered, "I know she's not a member of this committee, but I believe Carolyn would do that and if she did, it would be done right. Why don't we ask her?"

*   *   *

"When Edna agreed to serve as president, she had no idea her husband would be transferred this year. So, here we are, three months after we installed our new president, we're looking for her successor," announced Ruby Lawson to the other members of the executive committee of the women's organization at Trinity Church. "Any of you have any suggestions?"

"I know she's terribly busy," offered one of the ladies, "but if she will do it, I believe Carolyn would be an exceptional president. Maybe if we explain it's an emergency and only for eight months, she will do it."

"That's a great idea!" affirmed another member of the group. "Why don't we call Carolyn?"

While she seldom receives that award, Carolyn deserves the most valuable player trophy. Carolyn, and her counterparts in the churches across the land, deserve special mention. Every church needs several Carolyns, but rarely are they that fortunate. Thirty years ago the person most likely to fill that role was the minister's wife, but that was a long time ago in another world in a different galaxy. Who is the Carolyn in your congregation? If that question has an easy and obvious answer, do you love and appreciate her? If you do not have a Carolyn or two or three, where do you begin to look? Among the recently retired members? Or among some of your new members? Or is that lady who lost her husband six years ago a potential Carolyn?

Fixit Fred

"The south window in my office won't open and the door transmits sound so easily that everyone in the outer office can hear practically every word that's said in here," complained the new minister at Hilltop Church.

"Why don't you tell the trustees about your problems?" inquired Tommy Thompson, a good friend of the new pastor.

"I did the first meeting after I arrived, and that was two months ago, but nothing has happened," replied the minister.

"I'll call Fred and ask him to come over and take a look at it," offered Tommy. Two days later the window opened easily and that office door was neatly soundproofed.

"I got three bids to repair that leak in the steeple. The highest was $1,260 and the lowest was $940," reported one person to the board of trustees at Lime Ridge Church.

"That's a lot of money," exclaimed one trustee.

"I doubt if you will get a lower price," observed another trustee. "It probably means they're charging $700 for setting up the scaffolding, $200 for labor, and $40 for materials."

"If two of you fellows will help me with the ladders, I think I can fix that leak," quietly offered Fred. A week later the steeple had been repaired and Fred's bill was $26.81 for materials, but he did not bother to submit it.

Fred is another of those valuable players on the team at the middle-sized church. The best places to find a Fred today are in *(a)* farming community churches, *(b)* that shrinking central city congregation filled today largely with working-class members whose parents or grandparents came over from the "old country," *(c)* the county seat or small town church that draws its members from a wide range of vocations and includes many adults who are second or third generation members of that congregation, and *(d)* that new theologically conservative and rapidly growing independent church out on the edge of town that is attracting so many working-class people.

Sally the Scrounger

"What's this item of $100 for newsprint?" inquired one of the members of the Christian education committee at Oak Park

Church as they were getting ready to approve the final version of the proposed budget for the coming year.

"That's for these big pads of white paper we use in those metal easels," explained the minister.

"One hundred dollars for newsprint when people all around the world are starving to death!" exclaimed another member of the committee.

"They cost eight or nine dollars a pad," replied the minister somewhat defensively, "and that's after the discount we get from the store where we buy all our office supplies, and those are the pads with the cheapest quality paper."

"Why don't we buy those ends of a newsprint roll from the newspaper and cut them up to make the pads like we used to do?" inquired Sally Van Eck.

"The newspaper now recycles those ends, and they're not available anymore," clarified the person chairing the committee.

Two weeks later Sally brought a stack of 34" x 46" pads of newsprint into the storeroom at the church. As she was bringing the second load in, she encountered the pastor in the corridor.

"Where did you get these?" he asked.

"Made 'em," replied Sally.

"But I thought the newspaper was recycling those ends of rolls," questioned the pastor.

"They were," replied Sally, "but that West Side Shopping News does their own printing so I went out there, and they gave me two rolls. Would you open the door into the storeroom for me?"

*   *   *

"For ten years I couldn't show any filmstrips because my room faces the east and the sun came in so bright in the morning you couldn't see the pictures on the screen," commented the teacher of the third- and fourth-grade Sunday school class at Poynette Church to the Sunday school superintendent. "Last Sunday I walked in and imagine my surprise when I saw those heavy drapes on each of the three windows. When you close them, the room is almost completely dark. Whom do I thank for such a wonderful surprise?"

"Thank Sally," came the reply. "She heard you complain about the lack of drapes a few weeks ago. When her neighbor bought new drapes for her living room, Sally asked her to give the old ones to the church. She bought three drapery rods for a dollar apiece at the secondhand store, cut the drapes to fit, hemmed them, and last Tuesday she came over, hung them, took them home again, and rehemmed them after discovering those windows are not all exactly the same height."

"Last fall when I asked the Sunday school Board for dark shades, they told me the church couldn't afford them. Now we have these beautiful drapes and the only cost was three dollars for the rods?"

"Three dollars plus a lot of persistence by Sally plus I don't know how many hours of work cutting and sewing those drapes," clarified the superintendent.

Sally the Scrounger also is one of the most valuable players on the team of the middle-sized church. Her ingenuity, tenacity, dedication, and willingness to do a lot of work that is rarely seen and seldom recognized makes it easier and more economical for the typical congregation to carry out its ministry. The best scroungers have a strong depression ethic. Some acquired it by living through the Great Depression. Others inherited it from their parents and a few caught it from their spouses. It also should be recognized that many of the most effective scroungers are named Sam, not Sally. Occasionally they are addressed as "Reverend."

Three reasons stand out for lifting up the role and the contributions of these six personalities. First, as was pointed out earlier, a distinctive characteristic of the middle-sized congregation is the centrality of individuals. The small church revolves around families. The large church usually is "run" by committees, the officers and the staff, but those positions offered are filled by a passing parade of often anonymous individuals. In the middle-sized church personalities often are far more important.

Second, the usual table of organization for a church identifies such offices or roles as elders or deacon or Sunday school teacher or usher or treasurer or financial secretary or chairperson or lay leader or director. While the middle-sized church does need an organizational structure, and officers and committees are important, much of what happens in these congregations often is less the product of these official organizations and more likely the reflection of the perspective, values, commitment, or opinion of Uncle Harold or Katherine or Dennis or Carolyn or Fred or Sally (Sam).

Finally, the inflationary era of recent years has produced some serious financial strains on the middle-sized church, especially those averaging fewer than 160 at worship on Sunday morning. Carolyn and Fred and Sally, by their willingness to carry a far heavier load than that of the average volunteer, have made it possible for a huge number of churches to continue to be faithful to their call from the Lord. Carolyn, Fred, and Sally (Sam) rarely receive the recognition and gratitude they deserve for their commitment, their dedication, their willingness, their initiative, their loyalty, their creativity, their tenacity, and their boundless energy. This chapter represents an effort to thank some of them.

The other side of this picture is that the more prominent the role of individuals in the church, the more likely that congregation will see itself as simply "one big family." That self-image often produces what may be the most widespread obstacle to ministry facing the middle-sized congregation.

CHAPTER
FOUR

Act Your Size!

On a sunny afternoon in late April the thirty-three-year-old Rev. Douglas MacKenzie dropped by to visit Mrs. Anna Williams, a seventy-three-year-old widowed member of Grace Church. The minister was nearing the end of this third year as the pastor of this 246-member congregation, and it seemed as if the time he had available to call on people in their homes was getting scarcer every month, but he normally reserved two afternoons and two evenings a week for calling.

Shortly after the visit began, Mrs. Williams changed the subject with this comment, "I certainly do appreciate your coming by to see me, but I expect we won't be seeing much more of you."

"Why?" asked the minister. "Why in the world would you say something like that?"

"Well, I expect you'll be moving on to a bigger church pretty soon," came the reply. "Albert and Sarah Hawkins came by yesterday afternoon and as we were talking, we agreed you're the best minister Grace Church has had in many years. Albert commented that a little church like ours couldn't expect to keep a minister as talented as you are. Sarah said she expected you might even be moving on this year. I was sorry to hear that, but I guess they're right; some bigger church will discover you pretty soon and steal you away from us."

*   *   *

"That's the dumbest idea I've heard in a long time!" exclaimed Henry Balboni, a lifelong member at Trinity Church and one of the most influential members of that congregation. "Why would anyone suggest we go to two services on Sunday morning when we still have lots of room? Counting the choir area and the balcony we can seat close to 300, and we rarely have as many as 200 on Sunday morning. Except for Palm Sunday, Easter, Mother's Day, and Christmas Eve, we never come close to filling this place. Who suggested that in the first place? We're just a small church and most of our members would laugh at us if we proposed going to two services. The only place you see two services on Sunday morning are in big churches or perhaps in a new mission that simply doesn't have enough room to accommodate everyone."

*   *   *

"It seems as if every month the council meeting runs later and later," observed David Martin to his friend Hal Mansfield as they rode home together in David's car at 11:40 one Tuesday night after the monthly meeting of the governing board at the 305-member Pleasant Ridge Church.

"I'm afraid you're right," replied Hal. "When I agreed to come on the council, I was told these meetings were usually over by ten o'clock, but that's happened only once since I was elected, and it's usually closer to midnight when we adjourn than it is to ten o'clock. Last week I told the pastor that when my turn was up, she should look for someone to take my place. I have to leave for work at 6:30 every morning and I simply have to be in bed by eleven if I'm going to be any good the next day."

"This is my second, and last, term," declared David. "I've been trying for four years to get across the idea that we have to delegate more of our agenda to the committees, but no one listens. We have only three standing committees and Christian education is the only one that meets on a regular basis. The property committee meets on call and the finance committee has three or four meetings in the late summer and fall. Everything else falls on the council. That's why it takes us all night to get our work done."

"Yeah, and half the time we adjourn before we get everything taken care of," replied Hal in a disgruntled voice.

These three conversations illustrate what may be the most common characteristic—and also the biggest barrier to mission and outreach—in the middle-sized congregation. This is the tendency for the members of the middle-sized congregation to see it as a small church and to engage in counterproductive behavior.

This widespread tendency has three common results: (1) first, and most serious, it creates a self-perpetuating low self-image of modest expectations based on a perception of inadequate resources and limited potential; (2) the middle-sized congregation usually offers a limited range of programs, it often experiences an excessively high turnover in ministerial leadership, it rarely challenges the members to reach their full potential, and it frequently is underorganized; and (3) the combination of these first two tendencies has turned out to be the most effective single approach to turning the middle-sized congregation into a small church.

The best general response to this almost universal tendency is in the admonition, "Act your size!"

An operational translation of that advice is to preface most suggestions for innovations and proposals for new ministries with, "In a congregation as large as this one . . ."

A more detailed analysis of this issue can be seen by looking at the middle-sized church from two other perspectives.

The Lay Perspective

Very few of the laity have more than eight to twelve hours a week to allocate to the life, ministry, program, and administration of the congregation to which they belong.

Sleep, work, and family responsibilities fill most of the 168 hours in a week. Therefore it is unrealistic, and often self-defeating, to expect the typical members to look at the world from the same perspective as that of the minister. It also is unrealistic to talk about only one lay perspective. There are many. Frequently the widely discussed "lay-clergy gap" is far narrower than the "lay-lay gap." There are, however, a half dozen generalizations that do help one understand why the laity tend to underestimate the size, resources, strengths, and potential of the middle-sized church.

First, and perhaps most influential, is the very high visibility of those congregations with a thousand or more members. Their members usually gather in highly visible and impressive buildings and these congregations often include some of the best-known leaders of the community. These large churches dominate the public media, their ministers often are well-known community figures, and their special programs are highly publicized. By contrast, the 200,000 Protestant congregations that include *fewer* than one hundred people at worship are comparatively much less visible. Thus the members of the middle-sized parish naturally tend to compare their church with the more highly visible large congregations and, by comparison, conclude, "We are only a small church."

This use of comparison models for evaluating size was the reason one member boasted, "Our Lion's Club has 160 members and it is one of the largest clubs in the state." A few sentences later he added, "My wife and I belong to a small church on the north side of town that has about 300 members."

Second, in the typical middle-sized congregation there is far more going in terms of ministry, outreach, and service than meets the casual eye. Much of what is happening is visible to relatively few members. Nine-tenths of the members are totally unaware of the redemptive ministry that is part of choir rehearsal on Thursday evening. Ninety-nine percent are unaware of a particular visit by the pastor or a concerned layperson to a lonely member in a nursing home. The vast majority are not aware of the extent in which the dollars given for missions are utilized to expand the ministry of the universal church. Relatively few have ever looked in on the third- and fourth-grade Sunday school class. This lack of detailed firsthand knowledge about the scope of that congregation's ministry makes it easy for many members to believe "this is a small church and there's not much going on here."

Third, the typical career pattern of the most highly visible pastors is from a small congregation to a middle-sized parish to a large church. This causes many laypersons to view their congregation as a farm club that is training the future ministers of the big churches. This perception of role as a "stepping-stone" does not strengthen the self-esteem.

Fourth, a disproportionately small number of the ministers serving as bishops and denominational executives came to those positions from pastorates of small or middle-sized congregations. This pattern tends to reinforce the self-image of the large churches and undercut the self-esteem of the people in the small and middle-sized churches.

Fifth, for many members the highly visible program on Sunday morning conceals the range and variety of ministry that is taking place during the other 165 hours of the week. This leads to the old cliche about the pastor working only one hour a week and reinforces the notion of a small church with a modest program.

Finally, most members like to visualize this congregation as "one big family" and to support the notion that this is an "unusually friendly group of people who really love and care for one another." These values run counter to the idea that it really is a large and complex organization that includes a huge number of people with diverse needs.

These are a few of the reasons why the laity tend to underestimate the size, resources, and potential of the congregation to which they belong. In a world of big institutions the middle-sized church looks small to many of its members.

An Organizational Perspective

The admonition "Act your size!" has a variety of implications when the focus is turned to the organizational structure of the middle-sized church. From this perspective the differences between the small congregation and the middle-sized church are most striking. This fundamental distinction can be illustrated by examining several aspects of the organizational structure.

First, and most significant, most small membership churches operate on the principle of participatory democracy. It is possible to conduct a meaningful legislative session at a congregational meeting with 35 or 60 or 85 members present. It is impossible to have a productive legislative session with 200 of the 400 members in the room. This means that while the small church can function with a participatory democracy model for congregational self-government, the middle-sized church must utilize a representative system of congregational self-government.

A second and more subtle difference is a product of this first point. In every organization in a democratic society the people expect at some point to be able to appeal a decision made by a committee or group or organization. In the small church this frequently is the congregational meeting. In the adequately organized middle-sized congregation with several permanent committees plus a few task forces or special short-term study groups, the point of appeal usually is the governing body. Thus the finance committee prepares the yearly budget and it is received, and perhaps amended, by the governing board. If that budget is to be submitted to a congregational meeting, it usually is assumed that will be simply a matter of form. This is true of the recommendations from the Christian education and personnel committees, and other administrative and program groups. The larger the size of the congregation, the more likely the real point of appeal will be the central governing body, not the congregational meeting.

This leads to a third distinction among churches based on size. In the typical small membership congregation the members often come to the annual congregational meeting expecting to be actively and meaningfully involved in the decision-making process.

In the middle-sized congregation the recommendations have been formulated by committees and previewed by the governing body, and it is widely assumed the congregational meeting will "rubber stamp" decisions that in fact already have been made. This usually means the central emphasis in the congregational meeting of the middle-sized church might more productively be placed on fellowship (including perhaps a meal), inspiration, information-sharing, affirmation, recognition of faithfulness by particular lay volunteers, and looking ahead rather than on legislative activities.

The annual congregational meeting in the middle-sized church should be seen as having both a different purpose and a different format than its counterpart in the small membership congregation.

A fourth difference grows out of these first three observations. In the small membership church the governing board makes most of the decisions on administrative and programmatic matters. It prepares a budget, manages the property, reviews personnel, sets the Sunday morning schedule, decides on the priorities in mission and outreach, and acts as *the* central decision-making body. In some denominations the polity requires that all of these decisions be approved at a congregational meeting, but the job of the governing body is to do most of the work.

By contrast, in the adequately organized middle-sized congregation much of the *doing* is carried out by the appropriate administrative and program committees. The central governing body plans, sets the direction, determines priorities, serves as a point of appeal, resolves conflicts over resources, schedules, and priorities, reviews the recommendations of the committee, and approves the work of the administrative and program committees. Only on extremely rare occasions will the governing body of the middle-sized church feel obligated to "pass the buck" to a congregational meeting for the resolution of an issue.

This change from doing to planning and oversight usually means the monthly meetings of the governing body can be conducted in less than two hours if that middle-sized congregation is adequately organized.

This leads to a fifth distinction based on comparative size. In the smaller churches the hardest working lay volunteers often are expected to be generalists. One individual may teach a Sunday school class, sing in the choir, serve as church treasurer, and also be a member of the governing board. It also is widely assumed that person will know nearly everything there is to know about the life and ministry of that congregation and all that can be accomplished with an investment of six to twelve hours a week of volunteer time.

The larger the size of the congregation, the more likely lay volunteers will tend to specialize in one or two facets of congregational life. The church treasurer may know all about the finances of that congregation and serve on the governing board, but know nothing about the Christian education program or the inner workings of the choir. An investment of six to twelve hours a week, on the average, usually will enable that volunteer to know most of what there is to know about one or two areas of that church's ministry, but that investment of time means the person will be largely ignorant about many other aspects of the administration and program in the church. An investment of twenty to thirty hours every week is required to enable that lay volunteer to know about all that is happening in the typical middle-sized congregation and few volunteers can put in that much time week after week; therefore it is easier to specialize in one area of church life.

The small congregation encourages lay volunteers to be

generalists while the larger churches encourage lay volunteers to specialize.

This leads into a sixth difference among churches according to size. The basic generalization is that the larger the number of members, the greater the expectations the members place on the minister to possess an earned overall view of that congregation's life and ministry, to function as an initiating leader, to be familiar with all the details of every facet of congregational life, to be acquainted with every member's gifts and talents, to be omnipresent and, as a theologically trained person, to have an earned professional opinion on every subject. Since knowledge is a source of power, the larger and more complex the congregation, the more power the pastor will have.

By contrast, most long-established small membership churches are lay-owned and operated. The minister has relatively limited power by virtue of office. It is not at all uncommon for the minister to be only the fourth or fifth or tenth best informed person at the decision-making table—and in scores of small churches the minister rarely is invited even to be present at that decision-making table when it is in someone's home and only kinfolk and longtime friends are present!

One reason for this difference is the amount of time required to be reasonably knowledgeable about all facets of congregational life. Another is tenure. In general, the larger the membership, the longer the average tenure of the pastor. A third is complexity. The larger the congregation, the more complex its programmatic and administrative structure. A fourth is professionalism. The larger the organization, the more likely people will seek what they perceive to be professional counsel. A fifth is experience. The smaller the membership of the congregation, the more likely that church is being served by an inexperienced pastor.

A seventh difference between the organizational life of the small membership church and the middle-sized congregation is a conceptual difference. The 85-member congregation can be described as a congregation of 85 individuals and a reasonable expectation is that each of the 85 can call the others by name. The primary relationship of most of the members is to the congregation as a whole.

It may be more useful to conceptualize the 385-member church as a congregation of groups, circles, choirs, organizations, and cells. Every member of a Sunday school class can be expected to be able to call the other members of that class by name, but few of them will be able to call every one of the 385 other members by name. For many members the primary relationship to that congregation is to a Sunday school class or a Bible study group or to a choir or a job, such as ushering, or to an office or position such as treasurer, rather than to the congregation as a whole.

One implication of this is that an enhancement of congregational life as a whole should be a high priority in the small membership church. By contrast, the organizational structure of the middle-sized and large churches should be designed to affirm, reinforce, and strengthen each of the face-to-face groups.

A common consequence of this distinction is that a larger proportion of the members usually attend the annual meeting of the small church than will be the pattern in middle-sized and large congregations.

For those readers who, like this writer, feel a compulsion to count, an eighth distinction begins to appear when a congregation reaches 250 to 300 members.

Nearly every small membership congregation meets in a building large enough to seat every member in one room at the same time. A substantial proportion of middle-sized churches, however, meet in buildings designed on the premise that an occasion will never arise when every member will be present at the same time. One 280-member middle-sized congregation, for example, meets for worship in a room that seats 140 comfortably and can accommodate 210 in an emergency. There is a fellowship hall that will seat 110 people at tables and the next largest room will hold 25 to 30 people. This is adequate, except for Palm Sunday, Easter, Christmas Eve, and one or two funerals, for most of the ministry of that church.

If, however, that congregation expects to experience numerical growth, it probably will have to schedule an additional worship experience on Sunday morning and expand its facilities for the meeting of small face-to-face groups, including Sunday school classes. That may be relatively easy to accomplish, since most of the members affirm the importance of an expanding small group life in a numerically growing congregation.

If, however, this numerically growing congregation also plans to facilitate the assimilation of a significant number of new members every year, a greater emphasis should be placed on large groups and classes coming together and becoming better acquainted. These large group events also will help bridge the inevitable gap between the "early service congregation" and the "late service congregation."

One example of a large group event, which may include 150 to 300 people in attendance, is the New Year's Eve program that begins with a dinner followed by a fellowship period and a color slide review of the life and ministry of that congregation during the year just ended. If that includes a few songs, some skits, and a few other embellishments, it may run for two hours. Those present may next move to the sanctuary for a Watch Night Service and a fair number may return to the fellowship hall to celebrate the coming of the new year.

Other examples of large group events may include the annual celebration of the founding of that congregation, the missions festival, the hanging of the greens the first Sunday in Advent, the Saturday night square dance once a month, the father and daughter banquet, the all-church picnic, the June festival that celebrates the wedding anniversary of every couple who have been married five, ten, fifteen, twenty, twenty-five, thirty, thirty-five, forty, fifty, or sixty years, the congregational dinner at which the budget for the coming year is presented and members are asked to make a pledge or financial commitment for the new year, the annual meeting, the spring presentation of a religious drama, a choir concert, the reception for the new minister, and the rally sponsored by a committee of the regional judicatory high school youth group.

The growing 300-member congregation would be well advised to plan eight or nine or more large group events every year. This probably will not happen because *(a)* the building was not designed to accommodate large group events (other than corporate worship), *(b)* the program organization of the typical middle-sized church is organized around the concept of small groups, not large groups, *(c)* there is no one around, either paid staff or volunteer, who understands and appreciates the importance of large group events, *(d)* the congregation as a whole remains unconvinced that large group events in a growing church are sufficiently important to justify the investment in a fellowship hall that will accommodate *at tables* two-thirds to three-quarters of the membership, and *(e)* the system of governance created for that middle-sized congregation does not think in terms of large group events. In other words, it is naturally difficult for the middle-sized congregation to act its size.

This widespread tendency to perceive itself as a small congregation with severely limited resources also often results in decisions that undermine the financing of the ministry and outreach of the church.

How Do We Respond to the Financial Crisis?

"It's clear we're going to have to make some major cuts in this budget before we can submit it to the congregation," declared Sandy Wells, who chairs the finance committee in the 340-member Manchester Church. "Last night I spent three hours on it and came up with these possibilities. We could completely eliminate the $2,800 budgeted for public relations and advertising and the $3,000 for social concerns. I'm also convinced we can cut the music budget by at least $1,600, the Christian education budget by $2,600, the worship budget by $700, and the mission budget by $1,500. Those cuts add up to $12,200, and that's exactly the amount we decided two weeks ago we would be short this coming year."

For the next forty minutes the debate was over the magnitude of these cuts. The final compromise was to accept Sandy's recommendations on everything except in Christian education, which would be reduced by only $2,000 instead of $2,600, and social concerns which would be cut by $2,500 instead of Sandy's suggestion of $3,000. The remaining $1,100 would be offset by eliminating salary increases for both the choir director and the part-time church secretary.

What else could have been done? When Sandy Wells was challenged about the magnitude of those suggestions, the challenger was shot down with the reply, "You can't spend what you don't have! The only responsible action for us as leaders is to keep expenditures within the limits of our receipts."

A better response to the financial squeeze would have been to distribute the cuts among both administrative and program areas. The best response would have been to ask, "It appears we have to raise an additional $12,000. What do you think is the best way to accomplish that and when would be the best time to do it?"

That, however, would be difficult for many leaders to accept as a viable alternative. The finance committee of the typical middle-sized congregation usually thinks in terms of a pie that cannot be enlarged. The size of that pie determines the allocation of the financial resources and that is a fixed sum. It is difficult for many of the leaders to believe more resources may be available for a larger pie. This limited self-image is an especially powerful factor in those congregations that average between 160 and 240 at worship on Sunday morning, but that is another story and deserves a separate chapter.

CHAPTER
FIVE

The Awkward-Sized Church

Woodlawn Church was established in 1906 and for the next four or five decades it was clearly a neighborhood congregation serving a new residential community on the far west side of the city. A line in the official history prepared for the celebration of the seventy-fifth anniversary quotes an earlier minister who wrote in October of 1931: "Last Sunday we had 157 people here for worship, and all but eight walked to church, and three of those eight live close enough they could have walked."

By 1960 the city had grown in both population and area, and fewer than a third of the regular attenders lived within walking distance, and many of them chose to drive rather than walk to church.

The same man has served as the head usher at Woodlawn Church for over forty years, and he takes great pride in the fact that he has a ledger in which is recorded the attendance at worship for every Sunday morning beginning with January 3, 1943. He also has computed the average attendance for Sunday morning worship for each year. A synopsis of his record reveals wide variations over the years.

One night, after a Board meeting, three longtime members were sitting around drinking coffee and reflecting with the head usher on these statistics.

"If you examine these figures, you can see the impact a

pastor has on church attendance," explained Harry Anderson. "My wife and I came here in 1947. The church had been on a plateau in size all through the war years and following. We got a dynamic young minister in 1949 and attendance began to climb. Nine years later we peaked at 234. Shortly after he left we experienced a sharp decline. It simply shows what the right pastor can do. We got another crackerjack in 1971 and attendance went back up to a new all-time high in 1977. He was followed by a real dud we were stuck with for four years and attendance went down. Now we have a promising new minister, for only the third time since we've been here, and attendance is going back up again!"

"That's a great oversimplification!" retorted Jim Becker. "The times have a lot to do with it. Back in the fifties everyone went to church and our attendance went up. The

AVERAGE ATTENDANCE AT WORSHIP	
1943	135
1948	149
1949*	143
1953	207
1958	234
1964*	219
1969	163
1970	158
1971*	174
1974	208
1975	243
1976	231
1977	239
1978*	222
1979	203
1980	180
1981	166
1982	161
1983*	171
1984	187
1985	194

*arrival of a new minister

sixties were the years of the great disenchantment with all institutions, and church attendance went down all over the country. The seventies brought a new religious revival and church attendance is up again."

"What about that drop in 1981 and 1982?" inquired Betty Cochrane. "If it's the times, why did attendance drop in those years?"

"It was that dud we had for a preacher," shot back Harry Anderson.

"No, that's not the whole story," corrected the head usher. "I realize the competence of the minister is important, but in

1979 our choir director resigned. She had been with us for twenty years and had built up a big music program. My records show that in the 1973-78 period our attendance included an average of 34 in the adult choir. In addition, we had a youth choir that sang twice a month and two children's choirs that each sang once a month. In 1982 we had only the adult choir, and they averaged only 19 on Sunday morning for that year. When you count the parents who came because their children were singing, I expect the cutback in our choir program accounted for over half of that drop from the peak of 239 in 1977 to only 161 in 1982."

"Sure, and that reflects the difference in ministers," countered Harry Anderson. "The minister we had from 1971 to 1977 liked to sing and encouraged the development of all those choirs. The real reason Mrs. Ellis resigned as choir director back in 1979 was not because of her health, it was because she couldn't get along with that dummy we had for a preacher!"

"I just realized there are two other factors we've overlooked," commented Betty Cochrane who had been studying the chief usher's ledger. "First of all, we built the new educational wing in 1957. The planning for that and the construction created a lot of enthusiasm and reinforced a sense of unity. We finally paid off the mortgage in 1971, but paying off a mortgage is nowhere near as exciting as planning and constructing a new building."

"Yes, but that simply reinforces my point," interrupted Harry Anderson. "The reason we built that new addition was the enthusiasm generated by that minister. He brought in the people that made it necessary to build and he also promoted the whole idea pretty vigorously."

"The other factor we've overlooked," continued Betty Cochrane as she ignored the interruption, "was that from 1974 to the middle of 1977 we also had the benefit of a part-time director of Christian education. She did a lot of work around here that gave our minister more time for pastoral work. I think that had a big impact on our growth. She really was our program director and when she left to start her family, we never replaced her. No one has ever picked up all of what she did."

"But it all goes back to the minister," proclaimed Harry Anderson. "The only reason we ever hired her in the first place was because the minister knew her, recognized how talented she is and persuaded us to hire her. While we were thinking about replacing her, he announced he was resigning to go to a bigger church, and no one ever pushed the Board to fill that vacancy."

What Are the Characteristics?

This conversation illustrates several facets of what is truly a unique type of congregation. First, and most significant, Woodlawn represents hundreds of congregations that range in size between 160 and 240 at Sunday morning worship. Frequently these congregations fluctuate greatly in worship attendance. The reported membership may remain, more or less, on a plateau, but the worship attendance goes up and down. When all conditions are favorable, the attendance often is in the 220 to 240 range. When one or more internal disruptions come along, the attendance may drop to the 150 to 180 range.

From a lay perspective this often is perceived as a comfortable size congregation. The number of people, the competence of the lay volunteers, and the other resources are adequate for meeting most challenges. It is sufficiently large enough to respond to the basic needs for institutional survival and still have the resources necessary for a strong emphasis on mission and outreach. This size congregation usually can offer a diversified educational program for all ages. It often has a good ministry of music. It is large enough to attract and retain a highly competent and experienced minister. Usually it is able to afford the services of at least a part-time church secretary.

On the other hand, it is small enough that anyone who makes the effort can call nearly every other member by name. There is a high degree of spontaneity behind the genuine caring for one another. Comparatively few members feel neglected or overlooked or ignored. It is small enough to offer the intimacy and friendliness that so many laypersons place at the top of their priority list in seeking a church home.

From the pastoral perspective, however, this type of congregation often is too large and too complex today to be served adequately by one minister working alone without any other program staff. It is too large for one person to fill all the roles including preacher, shepherd, model of an adult Christian, youth director, evangelist, administrator, teacher, program director, tribal chief, parish visitor, prophet, priest, worship leader, cheerleader, chief executive officer, and resident planning director. Nearly every week the pastor feels frustrated because another Sunday has rolled around before every item on that list of things that must be done during the week can be checked off. The minister of the awkward-sized congregation would be far more comfortable if Sunday came around only once every eleven days.

Yet everyone knows and agrees, "We simply are not large enough to justify or afford a second full-time minister on the staff." This type of middle-sized congregation usually is too large to be adequately served by one minister, but cannot afford two. It is too small to have a full-scale program, such as one finds in the typical large church, but too big for the members to be satisfied with a more modest scale program.

Often it is also a highly vulnerable congregation. When everything is going well, the attendance may climb to the 220 to 240 bracket, but any internal disruption can reduce that figure by one-third. It is large enough to attract an impressive number of people, but frequently has an inadequate system for the assimilation of new members. The limitations of staff time and resources, a condition sometimes intensified by a change of ministers every three or four years, often mean that in this size congregation an excessive proportion of new members drop into a relatively inactive role within a year or two after joining. Typically it does not have the resources necessary for building in and reinforcing the redundant systems that would offset the shock of any one internal disruption. In a large church that extensive network of adult Sunday school classes or the music program with nine different choirs or the stability of the associate minister who has been there for eighteen years or that inspiring tradition of a great emphasis on missions or the network of adult Bible study groups or the carefully organized support system for the Wednesday meeting of the Youth Club often provides the momentum and continuity that enable that congregation to survive a major internal disruption with only a tiny drop in the level of participation. The typical awkward-sized congregation, by contrast, rarely enjoys the advantage of these stabilizing forces.

A second point that was illustrated by the conversation at Woodlawn Church is, Harry Anderson is right. The awkward-sized congregation, to a far greater degree than smaller congregations, often is highly dependent on the competence, compatibility, initiative, and tenure of a creative minister. Like many larger churches, and unlike most very small membership congregations, the awkward-sized church frequently is greatly influenced by the ministerial leadership. A good match can be remarkably productive. A mismatch can be highly disruptive.

A third point illustrated by the opening paragraphs of this chapter is that Harry Anderson is wrong. The awkward-sized church is too large and too complex to be explained by any single factor analysis. Jim Becker and Betty Cochrane are right. Many factors must be considered when attempting to analyze the ups and downs in the worship attendance at the typical awkward-sized church.

Fourth, the head usher is right. The awkward-sized congregation frequently can benefit from an extensive music program and also often reflects the depressing impact of a weak ministry of music. The basic generalization is that the larger the size of the congregation, the more important music is to both the religious vitality and the institutional health of that parish.[1] The typical awkward-sized congregation is larger than six out of seven Protestant churches on the North American continent and therefore the size and the quality of the music program may have a significant impact on the participation level.

A fifth lesson to be drawn from that conversation about Woodlawn Church was illustrated by Betty Cochrane's reference to the building program of 1957. As she wisely pointed out, that was an influential rallying point. The members were challenged. They responded. In addition to constructing a new educational wing, the folks at Woodlawn formulated and implemented a specific, attainable, measurable, highly visible, unifying, and satisfying goal. That not only enhanced the enthusiasm and increased the participation rate, it also melded the old-timers and newcomers into one congregation. Unfortunately, they finished that building and did not replace it with a new rallying point.

Finally, to go back to Betty Cochrane's last point, the awkward-size congregation frequently shows highly visible benefits from additional *specialized program* staff, but this is a point that deserves more detailed consideration later in the chapter.

The Conflict over Priorities

Bethany Lutheran Church was founded as a new mission back in 1964. Three years later what had now become a 285-confirmed-member parish moved into the first unit of their permanent meeting place. The impressive sanctuary was designed to seat 390 including the choir. The $385,000 building also included a large general purpose meeting room that could be divided with folding partitions to accommodate six Sunday school classes, a 12' x 14' nursery, the pastor's study, an office for a church secretary, restrooms, a combination storage-utility room, and an attractive central hall that was a comfortable "milling-around" area after worship. Despite a mortgage of $290,000 it was expected the second unit would be under construction within six or seven years. The mission developer left in 1973 and was followed by *(a)* a minister who was a genuine mismatch and who stayed only two years, *(b)* a pastor who announced during his fourth year that he and his wife were getting a divorce and he left a few months later, and *(c)* a dynamic, attractive, energetic, and exceptionally gifted pastor who arrived to find the morale very low, the mortgage reduced to only $245,000, the average attendance at worship dropped from a peak of 243 down to 160, and the Sunday school in a shambles. Before leaving for a denominational staff position, this pastor saw the worship attendance climb back up to an average of 192. The Sunday school was totally reorganized and doubled in size, the congregation began to discuss what was estimated to be a new $500,000 educational wing, and a satisfying rise could be seen in the level of congregational morale.

The current pastor is now in the third year of what everyone hopes will be a long, long pastorate. A long-range planning committee was created and at the first meeting these comments were heard.

"It seems to me that our immediate problem is to pay off the remaining $210,000 on that mortgage," declared a sixty-year-old man who was one of the four charter members still in a leadership role. "When we built, we had hoped to have the second unit under construction by the mid-seventies. We've missed by a good many years. If we can get rid of that mortgage, we'll not only save a chunk of money every year on interest, but we'll also be able to demonstrate to our people that we're ready for a second building program, and they will support it."

"I certainly agree it would be great to be free of the

payments on that old mortgage," added a thirty-seven-year-old mother of three, "but those of us who work in the Sunday school all agree our top priority should be on space for the Sunday school and a new room for the nursery. Even if it means a lot bigger debt, we simply have to have more room for the Sunday school. If this parish is going to grow, we must have better facilities for our children!"

"I expect I'm in a minority here," offered another member, "but there are several of us who believe we need to replace that old electronic organ with a new pipe organ. I'm aware of the crowded conditions for the Sunday school, but we've gotten along this far, we can make do for a few more years. Besides, it will take us several years to plan a new building and raise the money for it. I'm convinced there are enough people here who want a new organ that if we made that the top priority, we could have it paid for by the time it is installed. A good organ would add so much to our worship that I think we would attract more members, and that would make it easier to finance a building program."

"This may sound somewhat selfish," said the pastor, "but if we're building a list of priorities, I would like to suggest one or two additions. I need help!"

"What do you need most?" inquired one of the members. "What kind of help are you seeking?"

"I'm not sure what the best beginning would be," replied the minister, "but here are the possibilities. I need some help with my pastoral responsibilities. One alternative would be to find a semi-retired pastor who could pick up some of the calling, preach one Sunday a month, and also call on prospective new members. I had a great experience as an intern between my second and third year at the seminary, and it may be that we should look for a seminary intern who could work with the youth, preach once a month, help with the Sunday school, perhaps teach an adult class, and also do some of the calling."

"Which would cost the most?" inquired the member who represented the finance committee.

"Probably about the same," replied the pastor, "depending on how much time we expected from the semi-retired pastor. There's a third alternative that also should be on the list. That would be a full-time parish worker. My seminary roommate is the pastor of a similar size parish in Kansas, and he tells me that is the most productive help for the dollar that a church can have. I really don't have strong convictions on which would be the best direction for us to go here at Bethany, but I want you to realize that I do need some help. My family is complaining that I'm never home and instead of taking a day off every week, I may manage to take two days off a month, but some months it's only one."

"There's no question in my mind that our pastor needs help," declared another member of the long-range planning committee, "but as I've been sitting here, I've become increasingly troubled. Thus far everything that has been said has been about what we need to do for ourselves here at Bethany. I wish that mortgage had been paid off years ago; maybe we built too much to begin with. I agree the Sunday school is overcrowded. I would love to see us get a new organ, and I know our pastor needs help. But people are starving to death all over the world today. Millions of people don't have a roof over their heads. Millions have not heard the gospel. Right here in this community there is an acute need for more day-care facilities for the children of working mothers. Shouldn't our committee address those needs?"

These comments illustrate another facet of the distinctive personality of the awkward-sized church. It includes many members with creative and sound ideas about what that congregation should be doing in ministry, but the ideas often exceed the available resources. This same debate can be heard in the hundred-year-old awkward-sized church. The basic difference is that there the focus may be on renovation or remodeling rather than on new construction, on the cost of operating that huge building rather than on debt retirement, and on rebuilding an ancient organ rather than on purchasing a new one.

One reason the term "awkward sized" can be applied to this type of congregation is that the wants and needs often exceed the resources.

Before moving to some positive suggestions in planning for a new day in the awkward-sized congregation, it is necessary to examine six widely neglected concerns that often affect these and larger congregations.

The Organizational Structure

The first of these is the deployment of lay volunteers in general and the function and size of the governing body in particular. In most of the smaller Protestant congregations on the North American continent there are two strong pressures that often shape the size and role of the governing body. One is the concept of participatory democracy. The concept of direct democracy has a long history, and many smaller congregations pride themselves on the fact that "every one who wants to make the effort and invest the time can have a voice in the decision-making here." Sometimes this is accomplished by scheduling several congregational meetings a year. More often it means an organizational structure with (a) a large governing board that may include anywhere from fifteen to sixty members, (b) a modest number of functioning standing committees, usually finance, Christian education, property, and perhaps missions, (c) the temptation by the governing board to do, rather than to delegate and oversee, and (d) the tendency by the governing board to reconsider and rework every committee report.

It is unreasonable for the congregation averaging close to two hundred at worship to emphasize a participatory democracy approach to decision-making. It is impossible for two or three hundred people to gather and make intelligent decisions! In many awkward-sized congregations, for example, there is not a room in the building large enough to accommodate the entire membership at a business meeting.

Therefore, every middle-sized church should be operating on a principle of representative democracy. The congregation chooses a small number of members to represent the interest of the whole at the decision-making table. When a congregation has as many as three hundred members, there is little difference between 90 percent not serving directly on the board and 96 percent not being on the board in any given year. In both cases a few are making decisions on behalf of the entire congregation.

Serious consideration should be given by the leaders of the awkward-sized congregation to an organizational structure that includes *(a)* eight to twelve standing committees that meet regularly and carry out their responsibilities, *(b)* a high level of confidence and trust by the governing board in the work of these committees and therefore the board rarely feels compelled to rework a committee recommendation, *(c)* a governing board of seven to twelve members rather than a much larger number, *(d)* a clear understanding that the basic responsibility of the governing board is not to do everything but rather to make sure everything gets done, in other words, to oversee and to plan for the future, and *(e)* a willingness to ask *at least* one-half of the volunteers in this organizational structure to serve on ministry committees (missions, evangelism, worship, education, youth council, social concerns) and fewer than one-half to serve on administrative or means-to-an-end committees (finances, property, the governing board, personnel). It also may be wise to shift those strong-minded and activistic leaders, who always like to be "doing something today," from the central governing board to positions on program committees and replace them with future-oriented leaders with a more reflective type of personality.

One of the most serious risks encountered by the

awkward-sized church is that the means-to-an-end issues will usurp the agenda and crowd out the emphasis on ministry. This risk can be reduced by an organizational structure that challenges the majority of the most gifted lay volunteers to serve on ministry committees or in ministry positions such as a teacher in the Sunday school or a greeter or a counselor with the youth or as a tutor in a school or as a regular visitor to the nearby nursing home, as an evangelist or as a leader in the orientation class for new members. The "promotion system" should be to "promote" members from the finance committee to missions, not from the Christian education committee to the board of trustees. Too often the middle-sized church focuses on survival because the organizational structure places most of the influential leaders on means-to-an-end or administrative committees.*

Those congregational leaders seeking to develop an organizational structure appropriate for numerical growth in the awkward-sized church frequently will encounter four formidable barriers:

1. In too many cases the denominational book of church government prescribes the same organizational structure for every congregation.

2. All too frequently the pastor, who has spent several years serving smaller churches, is a strong proponent of a participatory democracy system and/or cannot conceptualize a different system and/or feels obligated to attend every meeting of every committee and consequently objects to the creation of more committees and/or refuses to accept the role of an initiating leader in creating a new system and/or believes very strongly that the central governing board should do everything.

3. A third barrier is that in some congregations in certain

---

*The classic debate on this issue has been going on in the Southern Baptist Convention for more than a dozen decades over whether deacons are called primarily to be ministers or administrators.

denominations, such as the Lutheran Church—Missouri Synod, the Reformed Church in America, and the Christian Reformed Church, the elders may see their basic responsibility as the supervision of the minister, rather than as doing ministry.

4. The fourth barrier is simply tradition. "We've always done it this way. Why should we change it now? If we only could secure the right minister and if we had a few more dedicated leaders who really loved the Lord, these other problems would disappear. The issue is not the organizational structure, it is the commitment of our people!"

In summary, the awkward-sized church is large enough that it needs an organizational structure based on the concept of representative church government, that affirms the role of committees, subcommittees, and task forces, that involves more people in ministry than in administration, and that does not require the minister to be present at every meeting of every committee.

Leaders Do Lead!

After an hour of heated discussion on a proposal to change from one worship service on Sunday morning to two, a member of the governing board at Trinity Church suggested, "It's clear this group cannot agree on a course of action. Why don't we set up a system to poll our members on some Sunday morning and discover their preferences?" Within a few minutes it was agreed this would be a wise move. The following month it was reported that the Sunday morning poll found 34 members in favor of two services and 119 in favor of continuing with one service. After that report had been heard, a motion was made, seconded, and adopted that Trinity continue with only one worship service on Sunday morning.

*   *   *

"Let's ask our members to identify what they believe should be the priorities in our church," urged the pastor at First

Church. "That's a good idea," affirmed one of the members of the Board, "but why don't we begin by asking people about what they want or need?" When the needs' assessment survey was completed, it revealed that by a substantial margin "more adult Bible study" was at the top of the list of perceived needs. The pastor took this very seriously and, a few months later, announced that a new adult Bible study class would be offered during the church school hour on Sunday morning and that he would be teaching a new class on the Gospel according to Luke on Tuesday evenings beginning with the second Tuesday in October.

The new Sunday morning class attracted two adults the first Sunday, three the second, one the fourth, and has not met since. The Tuesday evening class folded after four weeks when the attendance dropped from five the first week to three the second to one the third and none on the fourth Tuesday.

*   *   *

The thirty-three-year-old Forest Hills Church averages 185 at worship on Sunday morning and the paid staff is composed of a full-time pastor, a four-day-a-week church secretary, a part-time custodian, and a part-time organist who also directs the chancel choir. After nearly a year of study and debate the leaders of the congregation were ready to recommend that the paid staff be expanded by making the church secretary a full-time position, adding a half-time director of Christian education, and seeking a retired minister to come on the staff for a modest stipend to do calling and perhaps preach eight to ten times a year.

Just before this proposal was to be sent to the finance committee, someone proposed, "Before we do anything else, I think we ought to poll our members and see what they believe the new staff arrangement should be. After all, they'll be paying the bills, so they ought to have a voice in this."

An elaborate procedure was devised for this that allowed members to offer their opinions on the need for more staff.

When the results were tabulated, they revealed that slightly more than half favored making better use of volunteers and thus avoiding any increase in the payroll, nearly a third urged that if any money be spent for more staff, it should be allocated for a part-time youth director, and the rest were divided. Nearly one in ten favored the idea of employing a part-time minister of visitation, a few supported the idea of a half-time director of Christian education, a couple endorsed the proposal for a full-time church secretary, and only five members endorsed, without any reservations or modifications, the original proposal for the expansion of the staff.

* * *

These three case studies illustrate several of the consequences that often result when congregational leaders in the awkward-sized church refuse to accept their leadership responsibilities and seek to shift that burden by polling the members to elicit their views and opinions.

Before moving on to discuss why this is an important issue in organizing the system of church government in the awkward-sized (and also the large) congregation, it may be useful to identify four of the most common results of this temptation to poll the members.

The first is apparent to all who have survived experiences similar to these. It is frustration! The leaders work hard at identifying what they are convinced are genuine needs, only to find that their action proposals are vetoed by what appears to be either popular opinion or apathy.

The second result often is the perpetuation of the status quo. The members reject the idea of a second worship service on Sunday morning, only a handful register for the new Bible study classes, or the pastor continues to feel overworked as the additional volunteers do not appear to carry part of the load.

The third, and perhaps the most subtle consequence for the middle-sized congregation, is that this procedure usually results in a rejection of the changes necessary to enable the middle-sized church to move off a plateau in size. Each of the three examples cited here could be a part of an action plan for numerical growth in an awkward-sized congregation. Each one would be a logical component of a plan to expand the ministry in order to reach more people with the Good News that Christ is Lord and Savior. Each proposal has merit if that church plans to be able to accommodate and serve a larger membership. Each proposal has an excellent chance of being rejected if submitted to a popular vote.

A fourth characteristic of this approach is illustrated by the second example, the needs assessment survey. This is a popular concept, but frequently it *(a)* encourages members to identify what other people need, *(b)* misleads the leadership into believing the results measure an interest in participation, *(c)* results in a list of what the respondents believe to be the "right answers," rather than an identification of needs, and *(d)* produces such a long list of needs that sometimes the leaders are overwhelmed when they attempt to match the length of that list with available resources.

As was pointed out earlier, the last three decades have brought a rapidly growing demand for participatory democracy, for enabling the people to be heard, and for discovering what the people at the "grass roots" want. Therefore, it would appear to be only logical and reasonable to urge every congregation to encourage every member to be heard. Those are noble sentiments. Why does this approach so often produce frustration and block change? There are many parts to an explanation of that dilemma.

The first, which is a major theme in this chapter, is that the awkward-sized congregation is too large to function as a participatory democracy. It is unreasonable to expect all of the three or four hundred members to come to a congregational meeting every month or two and to make informed decisions. That simply is too large a group to legislate.

The second is that there is a vast difference between being heard and being heeded. The leaders of the awkward-sized church would be well-advised to open a variety of channels for the members to be heard. These may include suggestion boxes in the building, pastoral calls by the minister, cottage neighborhood meetings in members' homes where new ideas are presented for discussion and response, an occasional opinion survey sheet included in the Sunday bulletin, a system of lay calling in which every household is visited once a year, perhaps a public hearing on the proposed budget, the congregational meeting to discuss a new building or remodeling plan, letters to the editor in the monthly church newsletter, or simply the casual encounters between the leaders and the rest of the members. At least three-quarters of the discontent in the typical congregation is largely a result of that individual's conviction, "I have not been heard. No one ever listens to what I have to say." This distinction between opinions and instructions often is overlooked when the decision is made to poll the membership.

A third factor is illustrated by the basic concept of the needs assessment survey. To state the issue very simply, it is a bad idea. Most professional pollsters agree that it is somewhere between difficult and impossible for them to secure meaningful responses from people on what they want. If the professional pollsters find it unrealistic to identify wants or needs in face-to-face interviews with people, that raises a question about whether amateurs can achieve that result via a printed form.

It is possible to interview a group of individuals and discover where they say they hurt, but planning a response to that hurt is a responsibility of leaders. Interviews can be used to identify symptoms, but the leaders have the responsibility to translate that into the prescription that is the appropriate response to that hurt. When the patient says, "Doctor, I have a severe pain in my chest," the physician has to translate that hurt or symptom into a need or prescription. Rarely does the patient come in and state, "Doctor, I need triple bypass surgery." Likewise most successful Bible study programs are developed by leaders in response to specific hurts, rather than to the general plea, "We need more Bible study."

A fourth reason why polling the members often is not a creative part of the decision-making process in the awkward-sized church is reflected in one of the central themes of this book. The typical member of the typical middle-sized congregation believes it is really a small church. One of the tried and proved methods of turning the middle-sized congregation into a small church is to operate on the assumption it is a small parish.

This modest self-image often causes the members of the middle-sized congregation to think of themselves as "one big family" and their natural preference is to keep everything small and simple. Thus they will tend to oppose two worship services on Sunday morning, "at least until after we fill the building every Sunday at eleven o'clock," because that will increase the complexity. Many of the members will have difficulty understanding, Why do we need a full-time church secretary in such a small congregation as this one? Or, Why can't our minister do all the calling? Why do we need a second pastor? If an effort is to be made to survey congregational opinion, that effort should be preceded by a serious educational program to help the members grasp the nature of current reality.

A fifth reason why polling the membership tends to produce frustration in all sizes of congregation is that frequently the process is designed on the principle of one-person-one-vote that was enunciated by the United States Supreme Court in 1962 in the Baker v. Carr decision.[2] Too often the efforts to poll the members are designed to protect the anonymity of each respondent. That has obvious merit, but if the responses are perceived as "votes," the uninformed response is equal in weight to the informed opinion, the offhand response is equal to the thoughtful suggestion, and the peripheral member's opinion counts for as much as that of the most active leader.

A sixth factor raises a major philosophical question about

117

values. The issue is the merits of participatory democracy in the middle-sized congregation. Should the congregation with several hundred members attempt to use a system of participatory democracy for decision-making? As was pointed out earlier, a central theme of this book is that the middle-sized church would be well advised to act its size. It is simply too large to function as a participatory democracy.

Another facet of that debate is the issue of change. Back in the sixties it was widely believed that giving the people a voice would be an effective means of altering the status quo. Many years later one veteran of the confrontations of the sixties observed that it is ironic that the greater the emphasis on participatory democracy—with the idea that every group should have a veto—the larger the number of veto groups, and the status quo is the only course of action that cannot be vetoed.[3] Those interested in major change have found that the greater the power of each person's influence, the less likely that decision-making process will produce significant change. When everyone has a veto, the most attractive point for agreement is to maintain the status quo. The only people who do not have a veto on today's decisions are tomorrow's new members, the very people we are attempting to reach!

A seventh problem in much of the polling carried out by the churches is in the wording of the question. The issue can be illustrated by two examples.

While the process has been abandoned by most denominational leaders in recent years, one widely used practice in new church development was to enlist a group of volunteers who would go out on a Sunday afternoon and ask the residents, "Would you be interested in joining a new Presbyterian church if one were started out here?" Frequently that effort produced a disappointingly low number of affirmative responses and the proposal for a new church was abandoned. Or, in other situations an impressive list of prospective new members came out of that effort and these names were given to the mission developer pastor. The new minister quickly found that a large proportion of those persons were not interested in being a part of that new Presbyterian church he was being asked to organize.

A better question would be for the mission developer pastor first to make several thousand calls on residents of that part of the community. After repeated calls on those households in which the residents were not actively involved in the life of any worshiping congregation, the organizing pastor could ask these people to join their new friend in pioneering a new mission. The usual result of that effort is *(a)* nearly all of the charter members come from among the "unchurched," *(b)* most of them have not ever had any previous affiliation with that denomination, *(c)* they are joining their new friend, not a denomination, *(d)* they are more enthusiastic about helping pioneer a new mission than responding to a stranger's invitation in that Sunday afternoon canvass, and *(e)* it produces a substantially different list of names than does the Sunday afternoon visit designed to identify who would like to join a Presbyterian church.

The wording of the question, the importance of the person asking it, and the time it is asked influence the response.

Another illustration of the same point can be found in the relocation effort at the eighty-two-year-old St. John's Church. This 360-member congregation had been established as a neighborhood church shortly after the turn of the century. While the old building had a beautiful sanctuary, the structure was showing the wear and tear of eight decades of use, the space for Christian education was inadequate, the fellowship hall was the remodeled basement that also housed six Sunday school classes, and the off-street parking was limited to two spaces. After months of careful study the building planning committee came in with a recommendation that the congregation purchase a six-acre parcel of land, which would be closer to where most of today's members live, construct a new building on that property, and relocate. This was submitted to the congregation and rejected by a three-to-two margin. Four months later the same committee came back to the members with a different question. "If we are going to make major changes by remodeling or expanding the present structure, the city will require us to meet the requirement for off-street parking. This will require purchasing and razing eight houses, and the total program is estimated at $1.2 million. The alternative is to relocate. We estimate the initial cost at $1,000,000. If the congregation grows in numbers, as we expect it will at the new location, we undoubtedly will have to undertake a second construction program sometime in the future. Do you prefer staying here and spending $1.2 million or selling this property, relocating, and constructing new facilities at a new location?" By an eight-to-one margin, the members voted to relocate.

In both votes the question could be described as change. In the first vote the majority voted in favor of what they perceived to be the least amount of change. In the second vote it could be agreed the majority also voted in favor of what they perceived to be the less radical change. In the first vote the issue was perceived as radical change versus the status quo. In the second vote the question was one of radical change versus radical change. Frequently people will choose what they perceive to be the lesser degree of change, but sometimes the question is worded to mislead people into thinking the choice is between change and no change. Frequently that choice no longer is available. The real issue back at the Forest Hills Church was not what kind of new staff positions should be created, but between reinforcing the program with the possibility of continued numerical growth and dropping back to a smaller size.

The wording of the question influences what people perceive to be the real choices. If the real issue is between one form of change and a different form of change, the wording of the question should make that clear. One way leaders do lead is by accepting the responsibility for a realistic wording of the question!

An eighth and overlapping reason why polling the members may be counterproductive is illustrated by the relocation issue at St. John's Church. The typical congregational survey asks the questions, the members respond, the answers are tabulated, and the results are announced. That process omits one very important step. Most of us do our best thinking on the way home from the meeting. Therefore if a poll of the members is to be taken seriously, the process should include opportunities for people to express their second thoughts, to change their minds, and to take advantage of serious reflection. A simple way to do that is to schedule two or three congregational meetings to discuss the issue and wait until that third meeting to ask the members to register their opinion. The initial response to any proposal for change tends to be one of rejecting change. Give people a chance to reflect and poll for their second thoughts, not their initial response.

Finally, it must be recognized that when leaders ask people for an opinion, some of the respondents will read that as a request for instructions. What happens, for example, when the leaders submit a complex set of questions to the members to secure their opinions on the priorities for next year's budget? The proposals include a request for a part-time person to staff Christian education. Eighty percent of the respondents oppose this idea and perhaps a fourth of those understand the process to be a binding referendum, similar to a local referendum on an increase in the general property tax, rather than simply an opinion survey. Subsequently the leaders determine that it is absolutely essential that a part-time person be employed to staff Christian education. What happens? What is the response of those who mistakenly assumed this was a binding referendum on that issue?

The safe rule for congregational leaders is to assume that when people are asked through some formal process for their opinion, at least a few of them will understand they are being asked for instructions and will be disillusioned if their opinions

Likewise the more complicated the program and ministry of a congregation, the greater the probability of conflicts in the scheduling of various programs, events, and meetings.

In simple operational terms this often means that a calendar covering the next twelve months is sufficient for the congregation averaging fewer than a hundred people at worship on Sunday morning. The awkward-size congregation that is averaging close to 200 at worship probably will find it convenient and comfortable to think in terms of an eighteen- to twenty-four-month time frame. The big church, however, that averages four or five hundred or more at worship probably would be well advised to have a large thirty-six-month calendar hanging on the office wall.

When the factor of complexity is added, it may turn out that the relatively homogeneous and middle-sized congregation with a modest program located in a small town can operate within a twelve-month time frame. By contrast, the very large and unusually heterogeneous congregation with a large staff and an extremely complex program may find itself needing a forty-eight-month time frame.

In other words, the length of the time frame required for planning usually must be tailored to fit a particular situation if the people are expected to be comfortable with it. Too often the awkward-size congregation, partly because the leaders tend to underestimate its size and complexity, handicaps itself with an excessively short time frame for planning.

The second generalization is that age tends to influence how we look at time. The typical five-year-old is convinced it is at least seven hundred days between birthdays, while the nine-year-old feels it is closer to five hundred days and the sixty-year-old knows it is less than two hundred days between birthdays. The fourteen-year-old measures time forward from the date of birth while the typical seventy-year-old counts backward from the time of anticipated death. Three dimensions of congregational life reflect this phenomenon.

123

First, the younger the age of the members, the more likely they will see a goal that will not be attained for at least two years as being a long way in the future. Thus there is a natural tendency to be impatient, to focus on the *now,* and to think in terms of the immediate future. The older members know that two years is less than five hundred days away and therefore tend to be more patient and more willing "to postpone that until next year." This can be a source of conflict both in administrative committees and in program development.

Second, the age of the minister is a very important variable. The twenty-six-year-old pastor often sees a four-year pastorate as the norm while the fifty-five-year-old minister may remark, "Why, it takes at least three or four years to get to know the people and to be able to set your priorities. Anything less than seven years is really too short for a pastorate nowadays." Both of them are thinking in terms of approximately two thousand days as the length of an average pastorate, but for one that means four years and for the other that means seven years.

A third facet of the age factor is how long the congregation has been in existence. In the three-year-old new mission, many members become impatient when someone suggests it may be five more years before a particular goal can be achieved. By contrast, in the eighty-year-old congregation, where one-half of today's members have been for at least fifteen years, many people will be comfortable with a five-year plan for the construction of a new building or the addition of a second staff member or the paying off of the mortgage.

When these factors are combined, it is easier to understand why the twenty-nine-year-old minister may often feel uncomfortable with the twenty- to thirty-month time frame for planning that is appropriate for planning in many awkward-sized churches. What is the time frame for planning that you use for resolving the conflicts over priorities in your congregation?

Inreach or Outreach?

A fourth widely neglected concern that frequently surfaces in the awkward-sized congregation is on the criteria for setting priorities and for resolving conflicts.

In the typical small membership congregation a natural and predictable high priority is given to institutional survival and to "taking care of our own." This may not be commendable, and it is difficult to proof text, but it is a normal tendency in any institution that feels its survival may be threatened.

By definition, however, the typical long-established awkward-sized congregation has accumulated sufficient resources to be able to place a greater emphasis on outreach. The central importance of this issue can be illustrated by looking briefly at two very common, but often controversial, issues that surface in the awkward-sized congregation.

The first may arise in the proposal to hire a part-time youth director. Almost always the justification is, "We must develop a stronger program for our youth. We haven't had a good youth ministry here for years, and it's time we did more for our youth." Rarely is anything heard about reaching beyond the youth in our own member families. Experience suggests, however, that the churches that offer an excellent ministry with youth find that between one-fourth and one-half of the participants come from non-member households. The explanation is almost always the same. The youth from member families are so enthusiastic about the youth program they invite—and sometimes coerce—their friends to participate.

A second example is the debate over one or two worship services on Sunday morning. A long list of arguments can be developed to support the contention that the awkward-sized congregation should schedule only one worship service on Sunday morning. These range from conflicts with the Sunday school to dividing the congregation in two groups (usually it is already divided into three groups of those who rarely attend, those who attend occasionally, and those who attend frequently) to complications in the schedules for families if the children's choir sings at the first service and the adult choir sings at the second to the shortage of ushers. Almost all of these arguments are based on the desire to make things more convenient and comfortable for today's members.

An equally long list of arguments can be made in favor of a Sunday morning schedule that offers people two experiences in corporate worship. These range from being able to accommodate more people to offering people choices to enabling newcomers to help pioneer that new service to the fact that, on the average, four out of five churches that change to a two-service format experience a 10 to 15 percent increase in attendance to being able to plan different worship experiences for different segments of the population. Most of these arguments can be summarized under the word "outreach." The basic focus is on bringing more people together for the corporate worship of God.

Which arguments prevail when your congregation debates a proposal to change to a schedule offering two different worship experiences on Sunday morning? Inreach or outreach?

Small Groups or Large Groups?

The fifth of these distinctive concerns that separate the awkward-sized congregation from smaller congregations reflects the fact that the majority of adults have difficulty gaining a sense of belonging in a congregation that averages 160 or more at worship. Except for those who grew up in that congregation, it is too large to quickly and fully assimilate new members. The common response to that is to organize a series of small face-to-face groups. Many newcomers first "find a home" in one of these adult Sunday school classes or a circle in the women's organization or on the softball team or in a choir or a Tuesday evening Bible study group or as a member of the team of ushers. That response has considerable merit, but the awkward-sized congregation is too large for a series of small groups to be the complete answer. The majority of members simply will not participate regularly on a continuing basis in small face-to-face groups. The leaders of the awkward-size congregation need to be aware of the differences among small, middle-sized, and large groups and encourage the formation of various size groups. This point can be introduced by listening in on three common questions and the responses to those questions.

"When we were averaging about 100 at worship, we used to have between 18 and 24 people in the choir every Sunday," reflected a longtime member of one awkward-size church. "Now we're averaging well over 200, but our choir hasn't doubled. In fact, we seldom have more than 30 voices on any given Sunday. How come? Why don't we have 40 or 50?"

"When there were only a dozen or so high school age kids here, I wasn't surprised that we only had seven or eight showing up for our youth group," observed a mother of two teenagers. "Now our church has grown so much in recent years, and I understand we have close to forty teenagers, but the youth group still runs between seven and ten. I don't understand that. Why hasn't it at least doubled or maybe even tripled in size?"

"When we were averaging about 160 at worship, we usually had between 30 and 35 women show up at our monthly meetings," declared a veteran leader in the women's organization of an awkward-sized church. "Now we're averaging close to 240 at worship, we've added two new circles, but we still have only 30 to 35 women come out for our general meetings. I know a lot of the women now work, and that's why we moved our general meetings from the daytime to the evening, but why hasn't our attendance gone up?"

The answer to all three questions is the same. The size of the group reflects the central organizing principle. Most choirs in churches averaging around 200 at worship are organized around small group and middle-sized group principles and

127

the size of a middle-sized group usually ranges between 18 and 35. Unless that choir is organized around large group principles, it probably will not exceed 35 to 40 voices, even if the size of the congregation doubles.

A very common central organizing principle for the high school youth group is "we like one another and we like our leader." This small group model usually produces an attendance of seven to nine teenagers at the typical meeting, regardless of the number of youth in the congregation. If the group is expected to include two dozen teenagers, it needs to follow the organizing principles for creating a middle-sized group.

The "rule of forty" suggests it is very difficult for any group, no matter how many potential participants there may be, to exceed 35 to 40 at its regular meetings unless that group is organized around large group principles. That may be the most important single reason that the general meetings of the women's organization rarely exceed 35 in attendance.

In other words, while small membership churches usually can function very satisfactorily with a number of small face-to-face groups, the leaders of the awkward-sized congregation should recognize the value of *both* small groups *and* large groups. This means *(a)* an understanding of the concept of central organizing principles, *(b)* a recognition that many of the organizing principles and techniques that are appropriate and productive when used with small groups are counterproductive when used with large groups, and *(c)* a willingness to accept the need for large groups in the awkward-sized church.[4]

A simple example of this can be seen by looking at the large adult Sunday school class. The larger the class, the more important it is *(a)* for the leader or teacher to call everyone by their correct name at least once before, during, or after the meeting of that class, *(b)* to urge everyone to attend that occasional social event that enables members to become better acquainted, *(c)* to distribute a directory with the name, address, nickname, occupation, hobby, telephone number, and other distinctive characteristics of each member, *(d)* to remind every member by telephone or postcard of that special meeting, *(e)* to delegate someone to take attendance at every meeting and contact each absentee (or else some members will drop out and conclude, "They never even missed me"), and *(f)* to identify that class or group by a distinctive name (perhaps by placing that name on the door of the room, providing name tags or lapel pins, using that class name on the newsletter, or even providing T-shirts with that name on them).

In summary, if the awkward-sized church is going to fulfill its role, it probably will need a more complex organizational structure, leaders who accept the responsibility of leading, a longer time frame for planning, a heavier emphasis on outreach, and a greater reliance on large group organizing principles in music, youth ministries, the women's organization, the adult educational program, and other program areas. That leads us into the last of these six widely neglected concerns.

Staffing for Growth or Decline?

One of the most common reasons behind those fluctuations in attendance in the typical awkward-sized church was pointed out earlier in this chapter by Betty Cochrane's comments. This is the importance of program staff. Frequently the awkward-sized congregation is either understaffed or staffed only for better care of the members rather than for outreach. In several denominations, such as The United Methodist Church, the Reformed Church in America, the American Lutheran Church, the Lutheran Church—Missouri Synod, and the Christian Reformed Church, the normal pattern has been the understaffing of the awkward-sized church.

The congregation averaging around 200, more or less, at Sunday morning worship that is planning for a full-scale program for the assimilation of all newcomers and for significant numerical growth probably will need a paid staff, *in addition* to the custodial and musical personnel, of *(a) one full-time ordained minister,* (b) a part-time program director (unless the pastor accepts that role), *(c)* one full-time church secretary who is more than a clerk-typist-receptionist and ideally functions as the alter-ego of the pastor, and *(d)* if the pastor serves as the program director, a part-time specialist in some program area such as ministries with families that include young children or the assimilation of new members or leadership development or ministries with mature adults or ministries with families that include teenagers.

While there is nothing magical about this, some of the best part-time program staff persons come from that segment of the population who share these characteristics. They are not professionally trained for that position, they are mature adults, they are mothers, they do not want or need full-time employment, they love the church, they have a positive view of the world today, they like people, they are creative, they are hard-working, they are self-starters who can both motivate themselves and inspire others to participate, and they are not currently married.

Too often the staff of the awkward-sized congregation includes a minister (who occasionally may be a part-time student or concurrently serving a small church a few miles away), a part-time church secretary, a part-time choir director, and a part-time organist, although that often is the responsibility of a volunteer.

Those who are interested in a brighter tomorrow for the awkward-sized church would be well advised to consider this distinction between staffing for growth and staffing for decline.

A New Tomorrow

A central theme of this book is that no two middle-sized churches are exactly alike and the differences in the congregational culture usually outnumber the similarities.

Therefore any strategy for ministry must be tailored to fit the distinctive characteristics of that particular congregation. In looking at awkward-sized churches, however, a half dozen points recur so often they can be used as a checklist for those seeking to shape tomorrow.

1. The first, and perhaps the most important, is that the congregation averaging 105 to 160 at Sunday morning worship often can and should be conceptualized as a congregation of circles, classes, and other face-to-face groups. The leaders of the awkward-sized church, however, should see it as a congregation of *congregations* of circles, choirs, classes, and other face-to-face groups.

2. This conceptual framework makes it easier to comprehend and support the need for two *different* worship experiences on Sunday morning and perhaps two or three services on Christmas Eve. An expansion in the number of opportunities for the corporate worship of God may be the best way for the awkward-sized congregation to reach and serve more people.

3. This self-image also makes it easier to encourage a redundant system of adult study groups. Some may be organized on the basis of age and/or marital status, others by the subject, some by the hour the group meets, and a few by the point at which one finds himself or herself on that personal religious pilgrimage.

4. Martin Luther wrote that music is second only to theology in bringing peace and joy to the heart. A fair number of members of awkward-sized churches might even place music ahead of theology in their priorities.

The expansion of the ministry of music can be the most effective single avenue not only for enriching the peace and joy of the heart, but also for the expansion of the program, for reaching young children and enabling them to express their creativity, for the quick assimilation of new members, for expanding the group life, for a ministry with the developmentally disabled, and for creating a distinctive community image.

131

The larger the membership, the greater the priority that should be placed on a great ministry of music!

5. If the middle-sized congregation, averaging 140 to 180 at worship, is going to grow through the stage of being an awkward-sized congregation and grow into a large congregation averaging 250 or more at worship on Sunday morning, it is essential that the leaders recognize the nature of that sequence. That sequence is not simply "more of the same." It is more than simple change. It is a transformation into a new order of creation. This usually means the minister must possess far above average competence as a transformational leader.[5] It also means the congregation will experience a sharp degree of discontinuity, and a satisfactory transformation almost invariably requires an intentional effort by all the members to affirm the new. The natural tendency is to long to re-create that familiar yesterday rather than to face a strange tomorrow. Frequently this means the minister must challenge the members with the vision of a new tomorrow.

6. A new tomorrow for the awkward-sized congregation that is seeking to move into the large church category almost automatically carries with it a new leadership role for the pastor. These changes include *(a)* a willingness to work with a staff rather than alone, *(b)* a positive response to the congregation's need for the minister to be an initiating leader, *(c)* the capability to delegate rather than to seek to do everything or to be present at every meeting of every committee, *(d)* a sense of satisfaction, rather than frustration, with the increasing complexity of congregational life, *(e)* an ability to conceptualize abstract ideas, *(f)* an acceptance of the role of the number-one cheerleader in the congregation, *(g)* a recognition of the value of prefacing nearly every sentence with either, "In a congregation as large as this one now is . . .," or, "Given all the resources this congregation is blessed with we should be able to . . .," *(h)* a willingness to serve as the umpire-in-chief who declares the victories before some pessimist can label that event a defeat, *(i)* a strong future

orientation with an ability to plan at least eighteen to twenty-four months ahead, *(j)* an understanding of the distinction between gradual change and transformation, *(k)* an eagerness to involve new members in policy-making positions, even at the risk of offending some longtime members, and *(l)* a recognition of the value of redundant internal communication.

What If It Works?

Perhaps the most difficult question facing the congregation that has been fluctuating in size between 160 and 240 at Sunday morning worship for decades and now finds itself moving into the large church category with 250 to 300 or more at worship can be summarized in four words, "What if it works?" There are price tags on church growth, and these can be identified by examining the large congregation of today that has been transformed from an awkward-sized church into a large congregation.

Far and away the most common criticism by longtime members of what has become a rapidly growing congregation is that the pastor does not spend enough time calling on the members. This is what economists call a "fixed sum problem." The minister has only 168 hours in a week. Time spent on evangelism and church growth must be taken from some part of the week's schedule. The usual practice for the minister with an intentional growth strategy is to concentrate on prospective new members and hope that "next month I'll have some time to visit a few of the old-timers." Next month, of course, never comes.

In broader terms, one of the most difficult decisions for the pastor with a strong desire to facilitate church growth is choosing between the popular alternative of spending considerable time with the members or devoting many hours every week to implementing the new member enlistment program.

By contrast, the minister who is more oriented toward a shepherding role than toward evangelism comes to a different conclusion. "This week I must give a high priority to calling on several of our members who need attention, and next week I'll get out and call on some prospective new members." Both pastors often feel frustrated.

Perhaps the most subtle and the most significant price tag on numerical growth is a change in the leadership role of the minister.

The minister who has been trained to be the shepherd of the flock, always available and always responsive to every call, often has difficulty delegating both authority and responsibility to individuals and groups. Every committee sees itself as one of the two or three most important committees in the church. We can understand why the pastor cannot meet with every committee, and we can understand that it would be poor stewardship of time for the minister to meet with some of those committees that clearly are of peripheral importance. What we cannot understand is why our minister does not meet with our committee every month.

The delegation of authority and responsibility is one of the skills many ministers learn in order to facilitate a church growth strategy. This means a willingness to delegate *both* authority *and* responsibility. That often includes the authority to make a decision the minister might not wholeheartedly endorse. The slogan "I trust the people" must replace the desire "to be in on every decision."

This becomes a critical issue in the larger multiple-staff churches where the senior minister must become comfortable with delegating responsibility *and authority*. Some senior ministers are willing to assign responsibility, but reluctant to delegate authority. One measure of this is when the senior minister can authentically affirm and applaud someone else's initiative and creativity in launching a new ministry or program, rather than second-guess a better way to have responded to that need.

From the pastoral perspective the most painful price tag of moving from the awkward-sized stage into the large group category may be the creation of the AAOEL Club.

This club is formed by those *a*ngry, *a*lienated, and *o*lder *ex-l*eaders who are unhappy with all the changes that have been made. They complain they no longer know every other member, they are convinced the pace of the congregational life is too fast, they know this church cannot afford all these new programs, they are unhappy about the increase in the size of the payroll, they are overwhelmed by the new complexity, and they long for the good old days.

While their numbers rarely exceed 1 or 2 or 3 percent of the membership, the members of this informal "club" (it usually meets without prior announcement in a member's home) often can be highly vocal in articulating their unhappiness with the growing sea of strange faces they see around them in church. Anonymity has replaced intimacy.

Some ministers attempt to enlist potential members of the AAOEL in helping pioneer new programs and ministries, many simply try to "love 'em into silence" while others simply see this club as one of the inevitable price tags on an evangelism program that works.

Another very common price tag is illustrated by this statement, "If you want me to teach another year, you'll have to guarantee that no one else will be using my room during the week," demands the teacher of the second-grade class. This comment illustrates one of the subtle price tags that go along with the transformation of the awkward-sized church into a large congregation. Everyone wants their own turf. The choir wants their own rehearsal room. The lay volunteers are more comfortable if they have their own niche, the church secretary needs more privacy, the part-time choir director wants his or her own office, and the regular attenders at worship are offended, but not surprised, to find a stranger sitting in their pew. The larger the membership, the greater the security we find in having our own private place.

"I used to be able to keep track of everything in my head," mourns the number-one lay volunteer, "but now I have to carry a calendar and a notebook every time I come to the church." The larger the congregation, the more complex is the life of that fellowship. No one can keep track of everything without records and a calendar.

"What I don't like about it is that this church used to be run by the Board," complains an ex-leader. "Now it is run by the staff. I believe the church belongs to the people, not the staff, but I guess I'm alone in that anymore." The larger the membership, the more extensive the outreach, and the broader the program, the more likely that control will pass from the governing board to the staff.

"It sure costs a lot to keep this place going," grumbles the treasurer. "Our membership has increased by 50 percent, but our budget, after you allow for the impact of inflation, has nearly doubled." That is the normal and predictable pattern. The larger the size of the congregation, the higher the level of expenditures, on a per-member basis, and the higher the per-member giving for benevolences.

"What bothers me is the number of people who join our church, and a couple of years later they transfer their membership to another congregation," lamented another old-timer. "We must be doing something wrong. We didn't used to have such a high turnover in the membership." This reflects the generalization that the faster the rate of new members joining any one congregation, the more likely the percentage of members leaving also will increase. The comparatively stable 100-member congregation typically will lose four members in the average year. In the rapidly growing 600-member church, that proportion usually will be closer to 8 percent (deaths plus transfers plus dropouts plus other removals) and in the rapidly growing 2,000-member congregation the annual turnover rate often approaches 15 percent.

"Why do we have to have such a big paid staff? Why can't we use more volunteers and cut the size of that payroll?"

grumbles an old-timer. That, again, is part of the price of success. The larger the congregation, the more difficult it is to enlist volunteers. The larger the congregation, the larger are the size of some tasks that used to be carried by a volunteer. Now they are too large for one person to contribute that much time. The larger the congregation, the more likely it will be able to offer specialized ministries and programs that require specialized staff.

"My concern is that our membership is climbing a lot faster than our attendance," complains another member. "Back when we were a 300-member church, our Sunday morning attendance was equal to approximately 70 percent of our membership. Now we're an 800-member congregation and our Sunday morning attendance, while it has nearly doubled, is equivalent to only about 53 percent of our membership. What's going wrong?"

Although it would be wrong to offer approval of that trend, it can be identified as a normal and predictable pattern. The proportion of the members who share in the corporate worship experience on any given Sunday usually goes down as the membership goes up. The greater the depersonalization of congregational life, the less frequent the attendance by many of the members.

These comments are offered here, not to encourage the awkward-sized congregation to remain on a plateau in size, but primarily to illustrate that the preparation and implementation of an effective church growth strategy rarely solve a congregation's problems. They simply exchange one set of problems for a different set—and perhaps they trade for a better set. One component of that new set of problems usually is the need to expand the financial base, but that is a subject that also merits a separate chapter, for it affects churches of all sizes.

CHAPTER
SIX

Financing the Middle-Sized Church

The audience for a chapter on church finances in the middle-sized congregation can be divided in two groups. The first consists of what might be described as the "high-demand churches." These congregations place high expectations on anyone who seeks to become a member. Members are expected to be present for worship at least twice a week, to tithe, and to give that entire tithe to the congregation of which they are members. The denominations and congregations in this category usually expect a high degree of loyalty, support, obedience, and commitment from the members as well as a high standard of conduct in personal behavior. High-demand churches include the Wisconsin Evangelical Lutheran Synod, the Seventh-day Adventists, most Missionary Church congregations, the Christian Reformed Church, the Church of Jesus Christ of Latter-day Saints (Mormons), and those affiliated with the Conservative Baptist Association.

The level of member giving usually is sufficiently high in these congregations that this chapter not only may be of little interest to them, but also may raise policy issues to which many of their leaders would take strong exception.

The larger audience includes leaders from what might be described as the "voluntary churches." In these congregations the members who worship only once or twice a month usually outnumber those who are present at least forty-five Sundays a year. A substantial proportion of the members do not tithe in the biblical sense of contributing one-tenth of their income to the church, and a majority of those who do set aside a tenth or more of their income every year for benevolent causes contribute a substantial portion of that tithe to a variety of religious, educational, charitable, and philanthropic causes outside the congregation to which they belong. It also is not uncommon for the pastor to give part of his tithe to charitable causes other than the church which he or she is serving. An impressive number of the members of voluntary churches are regular contributors to parachurch groups and to television evangelists.

The members of the voluntary church are more likely to belong to other voluntary associations (service club, PTA, YMCA, garden club, 4-H, lodge, veterans' organization, professional associations) than are the members of the high-demand churches. It is not uncommon to hear a male member of the high-demand church comment, "There are three things that are important to me in my life, my family, my church, and my job." The man who belongs to a voluntary church is more likely to say, "I don't have enough evenings to go around. My job often takes up one evening out of the week. Monday night is football, Tuesday night I bowl, Wednesday night I go to my service club (or lodge or ?), Thursday night we go square dancing, Friday night we spend with the kids at some school activity, and Saturday night my wife and I go out to eat. It's hard to work in all those meetings which I should go to at the church." The voluntary churches usually do not require members to adhere to exceptionally strict standards in either their personal conduct or their religious life.

Frontier Methodism was a high-demand church. Of the first 650 Methodist preachers who were licensed or ordained before 1800, approximately 500 dropped out. Some were expelled. Many chose to marry and that usually meant leaving the ministry. In 1809 only three of the eighty-four preachers in the Virginia Conference were married. Today it is reasonably safe to suggest The United Methodist Church has joined the United Church of Christ, the United Church of Canada, the

Christian Church (Disciples of Christ), and the Unitarian Universalist Association in the ranks of the voluntary churches.

From the perspective of the Vatican, Catholicism is a high-demand church, but from the perspective of the person born after 1940 into an American Catholic home, it may appear to be a voluntary church. One facet of the great debate of the seventies in the Lutheran Church—Missouri Synod was over whether that denomination should be a high-demand or a voluntary church and also over who would define the standards if it was to continue as a high-demand church. Some of the leaders of the Southern Baptist Convention have decided to replay that same scenario during the eighties. Traces of a parallel debate can be found in the Reformed Church in America, among the more conservative branches of the Amish-Mennonite family and in several of the smaller Baptist denominations.

This chapter is addressed to leaders of what can be described as the voluntary churches. The suggestions on financing the life, ministry, and outreach of the middle-sized church rest on several assumptions that deserve thoughtful consideration.

Basic Assumptions

The most important of these seven assumptions, and the one that will receive the most resistance from many readers, is that stewardship is not the issue. The churches have done a far better job of teaching stewardship than they give themselves credit for doing. The evidence for that assertion is all around us. It includes the increase in the proportion of churchgoers who give, the increase in the proportion of the average churchgoer's income that is allocated to religious causes,[1] the huge quantities of money mailed to the television evangelists, the increase in the number of corporations that assign a percentage of their annual profits to charitable causes, the receptive climate for the expansion of the environmental movement, the growth of the United Appeal and the response by Americans to a huge number of charitable causes publicized by the newspapers and radio every day of the year.

This is not to suggest an end to stewardship education. Every congregation represents a parade of people passing through that parish; therefore a continuing stewardship education effort is necessary to reach each generation of newcomers.

The second assumption is a simple diagnostic statement. The real reason most congregations experiencing financial difficulties are in that plight is not because of the poor stewardship of the members. More often than not the leaders have failed to communicate effectively to the members the financial needs of that congregation. A variety of other attractive causes are competing for each member's tithe. These range from church-related colleges and children's homes to radio and television preachers to direct-mail appeals for world hunger to solicitors knocking on doors to the financial needs of the other voluntary organizations to which that member belongs. A variety of studies by organizations engaged in fund-raising suggests that the average churchgoing family contributes approximately two-thirds of its annual charitable contributions to religious agencies and one-third to other causes. Conversations with hundreds of parish leaders also support this second assumption. The typical member of the voluntary-type church gives to a variety of causes, and one reason for that is not disloyalty, but simply a more persuasive appeal from these other causes.

The American Association of Fund-Raising Council, Inc., reports a total of more than 300,000 charitable organizations, institutions, and agencies in the United States dedicated to helping those who are least able to help themselves. In 1984 approximately $67 billion was contributed to charitable causes, slightly less than one-half of which was for religious agencies. There is a lot of competition for the philanthropic dollar and some of those competitors are exceptionally skillful communicators!

141

The third assumption is the easiest to document statistically. There is a lot of money out there! After allowing for the erosion of the dollar because of inflation, the private net worth of the American people tripled between 1950 and 1983. During the 1970-82 period Americans age sixty-five and over (persons age sixty-five and over are twice as likely to be in church on the average Sunday as persons in the under-thirty age bracket) were the only age cohort to experience an increase in both income and accumulated wealth that exceeded the rate of inflation.[2] In 1980 the federal government began to report how much money was placed by individuals in special savings accounts and investments for their retirement years. In 1981 the total was $26 billion. Two years later the amount set aside that year for retirement had tripled to $80 billion.

The fourth assumption runs completely counter to conventional wisdom. The conventional wisdom states, "If we go into a building program, that will mean a decrease in the giving for our operating budget and benevolences." Or, "If we begin to charge our members for tuition for their children who are enrolled in our Christian Day School, the parents will simply decrease the amount they contribute to the parish by the amount of the tuition." Or, "Sure, we can go ahead with that special appeal that is being proposed, but the members who give to that will decrease the amount they pledge next year because they will be expecting to be hit with another special appeal." Those statements are based on a fixed-sum concept of the economic world. Study after study has revealed that giving is habit-forming. People who gave to one cause are the ones most likely to give to another cause. The basic generalization is that requests for second-mile designated giving produce contributions that church otherwise would not receive.

The fifth assumption is the easiest to articulate. The best means of raising money in the church is to ask people to contribute. Most of the churches that are experiencing severe financial problems have had an inferior system for asking the members for money.

The sixth assumption is that many people will give more to what they perceive to be a worthy cause if they have time to talk themselves into giving more. Too often the leaders in the churches approach members, explain a particular need, and ask for an immediate response. Many people will give more if given a chance to talk themselves into it.[3]

Finally, and this is the most complex and perhaps the most controversial of these assumptions, the unified budget is an obsolete concept. It was a casualty of the longest inflationary era in American history. The concept of a unified budget, which includes in one annual asking all of a congregation's financial responsibilities for missions, mortgage payments, local expenses, and building maintenance, flourished in the years following the end of World War II. The dream was that a unified budget would eliminate, or at least sharply reduce, all those special offerings for specific causes. Combining the benevolence budget and the building fund with the local budget would mean that the members would be asked to make only one financial pledge for the coming year that would cover all needs. It would mean one financial drive, one treasurer, and one treasury. That would cover all the members' giving. It would eliminate all of those scattered funds, each with its own treasurer. It would be neat, efficient, and more businesslike. It would eliminate the competition among the various funds and needs. The budget preparation committee, with an overall view of all the needs, could set the priorities and allocate the resources accordingly.

In thousands of congregations this became the goal and it was achieved. With the exception of the women's organization, the youth fellowship, one or two adult Sunday school classes, and perhaps three or four special financial appeals at Easter, Christmas, Thanksgiving, and other occasions, all the giving of the members was channeled through that central treasury and reported as a part of the unified budget.

Gradually, however, various forces began to erode the

concept of a unified budget. The first big one was the building fund drive. Everyone in the congregation agreed that if we were going to be able to construct the proposed new building, we could not finance it out of the unified budget. There would have to be a special financial campaign. Several years later, after perhaps the second or third building fund drive, the remaining years of mortgage payments were consolidated into the unified budget. This produced a modest squeeze in other items in the budget, particularly benevolences and salaries, but the goal of a unified budget prevailed.

A more modest erosion of the concept can be traced back to the beginning when it was agreed that all expenditures would be included in that unified budget, "except, of course, the special offerings at Christmas, Easter, and Thanksgiving." Gradually the list of approved, or at least acceptable, special offerings grew from three to four to five or to six to perhaps eight or ten.

In several denominational families the most obvious departure from the concept came when the decision was made to launch a major denominational financial drive for missions or ministerial pensions or a church-related college or an expansion of the camping facilities or a home for the elderly or a theological seminary or black colleges. These multimillion-dollar campaigns usually (*a*) were conducted outside the unified budget of both the regional judicatory and the congregations, (*b*) met or exceeded the goal, and (*c*) caused at least some leaders to reconsider the merits of special appeals.

One of the most significant factors was the emergence of what one research project termed, "The New Audiences."[4] This study pointed out that the new generation of church members was less motivated in their giving than previous generations by such factors as guilt, fear of God, social pressure, or habit. This new generation seeks a voice in the decisions on the allocation of resources. Designated or second-mile giving is one way the laity feel they have a voice in the allocation of resources.

Further erosion of the concept came with the inflationary wave that began in the mid-sixties. In the twenty years between 1947 and 1967 the buying of power of the American dollar dropped by one-third. During the next seventeen years the longest inflationary era in American history eroded two-thirds of the buying power of the dollar.

In an inflationary era most people seriously underestimate their own income. As a whole, Americans report a higher family income figure to the Internal Revenue Service than they do to the Census Bureau. Most people calculate their total income only once a year and that is early in the calendar year when they prepare to file an income tax return. The typical Protestant congregation asks members in the fall to make a financial commitment for the coming calendar year, but that commitment often is based on that member's recollection of her or his income for the previous year. In the fifties, when the inflationary rate was approximately 1 percent per year, that two-year lag was of minor significance. During the inflationary years of the past decade that two-year lag ranged from 8 to 26 percent.

Overlapping that is the increase in the pessimism about the future. Today's adults are less optimistic about the future than were their counterparts of twenty-five years ago when the idea of a unified budget flourished.[5] Many people are more open to giving *now* than to making a commitment on their income in an uncertain future.

Finally, the increase in the level of the economic well-being of the vast majority of the people has undermined the concept of asking people to make a pledge out of anticipated future income toward a unified budget. Millions of people give out of current income to the operating budget of the congregation to which they belong, and, if asked, they will give out of accumulated savings to a capital funds drive, whether it be congregational or denominational. This pattern is an increasingly common phenomenon. It can be seen most clearly in those congregations that have experienced a severe squeeze

145

in their operating budget, but a special appeal for missions or to repair the roof or to support ministerial pensions or to install a new organ or to fund a scholarship program quickly is oversubscribed. It appears that many church members give out of that right hand pocket of current income to the congregation's annual budget. When asked, they dig into that left hand pocket of accumulated savings to respond to a major mission appeal or for some other attractive cause.

Thousands of congregations, however, assume that left hand pocket is empty and are frustrated when the income from the right hand budget is insufficient for the needs identified in the unified budget. The emergence of a fat left hand pocket among 60 percent of American adults has completed the process of making the unified budget into an obsolete concept.

What Are the Alternatives?

If the concept of a unified budget has been eroded by a changing economic and cultural context, what alternatives are open to congregational leaders as they face needs that are rising more rapidly than the increase in member giving?

The easiest plan of action, of course, is to pretend the changes identified here have not occurred and to continue with the traditional once-a-year appeal to finance the unified budget. This may result in decreasing expenditures for programs, benevolences, and salaries, but the ideal of a unified budget can be retained.

In other congregations the present approach to a unified budget is working, and no one is worried, so don't try to fix what isn't broken!

A more attractive alternative to many ministers will be to focus on a strong stewardship education program that encourages more members to tithe and to give that entire tithe to the congregation of which they are members. In those congregations with an effective teaching ministry this can be a productive course of action. In others it should be seen as a long-term strategy and may mean surviving several lean years until that educational program produces a significant increase in the giving level. This is an attractive alternative in those congregations with the expectation of a long pastorate or in those churches that are in the process of transforming themselves into high-demand congregations.

A third alternative is to shift to a July 1 to June 30 (or June 1 to May 31) fiscal year and to schedule the stewardship emphasis or every-member visitation to a more favorable—and more optimistic—time of year. In general, it is better to ask people for money (*a*) when the days are getting longer, and they are more optimistic about the future, rather than when the days are getting shorter and people are more pessimistic, (*b*) shortly after they have made out their federal income tax return and thus have a realistic understanding of their total income, (*c*) in the north, when the weather is turning warm, rather than when it is turning cold and a severe winter may be just ahead, (*d*) after Christmas, when people have paid their Christmas bills, rather than in November when the national media regularly predict dire economic news for the nation, (*e*) just before the beginning of a new program year rather than shortly after the beginning of the current program year, (*f*) in most congregations (except perhaps in Florida, Arizona, Michigan, Minnesota, Washington, and Oregon where the weekend vacation season already has begun) on Mother's Day, and (*g*) after that big annual celebration of the resurrection of our Lord, but before the members begin to leave for weekend trips and vacations.

A fourth alternative is to shift from the ministerial perspective, which usually emphasizes stewardship as a life-style for the Christian, and to accept the fact that a substantial majority of the laity prefer designated second-mile giving over a unified budget. This means a radical change in the basic agenda from stewardship education to fund raising! That change, which often is a part of the financial base of scores of high-demand churches, usually raises the anxiety level of the leaders in the voluntary churches.

147

Under this fourth alternative are a huge variety of approaches to fund raising, but two deserve the serious consideration of leaders in the voluntary churches.

The Wish List

A group of volunteers at Trinity Church was assembling the annual Wish List booklet. Two volunteers were busy collating the sheets while another was stapling and two others were stuffing and sealing the envelopes.

As they worked, John Harrison, a seventy-one-year-old widower, exclaimed, "I never knew they needed a piano for the third- and fourth-grade Sunday school room. If someone had told me they needed one, I would have given them mine. I have a perfectly good piano sitting in our living room. I bought it for my wife on her sixtieth birthday. Three years later she died, and it's been sitting there ever since. Our kids all live so far away it would be too expensive to move it. It probably needs tuning, but I'm sure if my wife were here now, she would be delighted to see it used in the Sunday school. I'll even pay to have it tuned if we can get a group of men together to help move it."

The reason for Mr. Harrison's offer was that the top half of page nine of the new Wish List booklet described that need. The two members who were the team teachers for the third- and fourth-grade Sunday school class had submitted that wish. It was described in three brief paragraphs at the top of page nine in this 5½" x 8½" booklet. As he was helping to assemble these sixteen-page booklets, Mr. Harrison's attention had been called to that wish.

Mature readers will recall that the term "wish book" was a synonym applied to the Sears, Roebuck catalog back before this became an affluent society. Children would spend hours perusing the colorful pages of clothes and games. Television now stimulates many of the wishes of children—and adults.

At Trinity Church a new version of the wish book was

created as a result of the longest inflationary era in American history. Year after year the leaders responsible for preparing the budget were forced to eliminate several requests in order to make the proposed expenditures match the anticipated income. Those deletions produced frustration among many members who saw their favorite ideas either underfinanced or not included in the budget. Finally someone suggested the concept of the wish book.

The first year the result was simply a list, printed on one side of one sheet of paper that listed several needs that, for one reason or another, were not included in the budget. By the fourth year the concept had evolved into the 5½″ x 8½″ booklet printed on an offset press. It included black-and-white photographs or simple line drawings of many of the needs. Mr. Harrison's eye had been caught by the sketch of a piano at the top of page nine.

A member of Trinity had designed an attractive cover page and the back page provided a form to be torn out and filled in by anyone who could fulfill a wish. The inside fourteen pages carried a total of four dozen wishes. These ranged from the piano for the third- and fourth-grade rooms to another volunteer to help with the nursery to a set of five dozen cups and plates for serving snacks to a television receiver for an anonymous shut-in member to thirty additional hymnals for the sanctuary to repainting the fellowship hall to a desk and chair to be placed in the classroom used by lay volunteers during the week to several trees to be planted in the churchyard to a set of dark shades that would enable the teacher to show slides and movies in the junior high room to racks for the storage of name tags when members leave the building to $1,000 toward a new well for a village in Zaire to a new power hedge trimmer for use by the volunteer garden group that takes care of the landscaping at the church to a window air-conditioner for the nursery to requests for the donation of food for the local "Common Pantry" that responds to emergency requests to a new carpet in the kindergarten

149

room to household goods to be used by the committee that was helping to resettle Asian refugees.

Many of the wishes carried a price tag with the expectation the donor(s) would contribute the money necessary to fulfill that wish. Other wishes did not carry a dollar sign; it was presumed a person or group would be able to contribute that item or provide that service.

"Every year we see two contradictory patterns," explained the pastor when asked about Trinity's experience with the Wish List. "Every fall the budget committee finds it has to reduce the requested expenditures. In February we publish the Wish List catalog. By the end of July we usually have some cash flow problems, because of the summer slump in attendance, but most of the wishes have been fulfilled and completely paid for."

"Does that mean that people divert their giving from the regular budget to finance some of the items in the Wish List?"

"We have absolutely no evidence of that," came the quick reply. "I've been the pastor here for fifteen years, and we've always had a cash flow problem during the summer slump. It's no more of a problem today than it was before we began the Wish List. The big difference is now we receive an extra $10,000 to $15,000 a year in cash for items that were squeezed out of the budget. Sometimes the church receives the item requested rather than the cash."

Why would your congregation want to produce a Wish List every year? Experience suggests at least three reasons. First, many members are attracted by the idea of designated second-mile giving. *The North American Interchurch Study* reported that 40 percent of the laity in the United States and 30 percent of the laity in Canada believe people will give more generously if they can designate the way the money is to be spent. Some people will make an extra contribution if they can be sure of how the money will be used. A second reason is that it can match needs and resources. Mr. Harrison did not know of the need for a piano until he saw it in the catalog. Third, it provides a redundant or "back-up" system for financing the needs of the congregation. What is not covered through the regular budget may be picked up through the Wish List. The use of the catalog provides a back-up system for the frustrated member who is unhappy because a strongly desired need was deleted from the budget. If no one picks it up from the Wish List, that suggests there was a lack of broad support for that need.

Perhaps the most common objection is rarely heard out loud. "Why should Bill Smith receive such an overwhelmingly public expression of gratitude for purchasing a $300 carpet when I give ten times that amount to the regular budget and no one ever thanks me for my contribution?"

An overlapping objection is the widely shared, but undocumented belief described earlier that second-mile designated giving undercuts the regular budget and/or the belief that a congregation should have only one system for contributions and only one appeal for the financial support of the life, ministry, and outreach of that parish. Although there is no evidence that second-mile giving will have a negative impact on the budget, those who are convinced this is a fixed-sum society believe it is certain to happen.

A third objection is, "How can you turn down the offer of a piano that no one would pay $10 for, but the donor is a loyal member who might be offended if we don't take it?" The answer, of course, is to have a committee that examines every potential gift to determine if it will fulfill the need.

A fourth objection concerns bookkeeping. "It's easy to give someone a receipt for $500 in response to a cash gift, but how can you give a receipt for tax purposes for a second-hand piano?" The answer is that thousands of non-profit organizations have been doing that for years. It is a skill that can be learned.

A fifth objection is that it undermines the authority of the budget committee or the governing board. If they determine it would be unwise to spend money on a particular need or cause, the use of the Wish List enables a few people to override that decision. Essentially this boils down to a conflict over power and control.

A parallel system used by a few congregations is to dispense with the list or catalog. Instead, these congregations post on the walls in the most heavily used corridor or room in the building pictures and sketches of needs that have not yet been financed. An Episcopal parish in Florida, for example, posted on a wall in a corridor sketches of the needs for the renovation and expansion of their building. A few years later that parish received an unexpected bequest that covered the full cost of a new chapel. Pictures do communicate better than words! Let the people see the unmet needs.

If you are completely satisfied with the financial support your members provide for your congregation, stop reading this and express to God your gratitude. If some needs are not being met in your congregation and if resources appear to be available but are not being offered, you may want to consider this approach. If the budget committee felt obligated to eliminate some requests in order to match anticipated giving, you may want to consider this idea.

If you are in a congregation in which no member is able to purchase a new automobile, no one owns a home video recorder, no one can afford a vacation out-of-state, no one has a home movie camera, no one collects antique furniture, no one has air-conditioning in their home, and no family is able to send their children to a private college, this concept of encouraging designated second-mile giving may not fit your parish.

Do you believe a Wish List, or some variation on that concept, might enable your congregation to expand its program and outreach? If you do, the critical question is, Do you believe this approach would be consistent with the values and goals of your congregation?

Miracle Sunday

The value of designated second-mile giving as a means of expanding the financial base is being utilized increasingly, but usually the total amount received is equivalent to 25 percent or less of the regular budget. Occasionally a congregation needs a much larger amount of supplemental income. The traditional approach, for example, in the congregation confronted with the need to construct a $300,000 addition to the meeting place has been to launch a building fund campaign in which the members are asked to make second-mile pledges to that project over two or three years. Some gave out of accumulated savings, many gave out of current income.

Today, with the tremendous increase in the quantity of accumulated wealth of 60 percent of the adult population, more and more churches are turning to that left hand pocket and asking members to contribute out of their savings as well as out of their current income. What this approach consists of, very simply, is raising a very large amount of money, nearly all of it in cash, on one Sunday.

Typically the amount received is equivalent to between one-third and three times the combined total for the operating budget and benevolences. For example, on December 16, 1979, a downtown church in Muncie, Indiana, with an operating budget of $335,000 received $1,120,000 in cash. A Lutheran parish in rural Iowa with an annual budget of $42,000 received $47,000 in the space of eight days. Scores of churches, including a large number in Texas and Florida, have received over a million dollars on one Sunday. If the amount sought is less than an amount equal to one-third of the normal annual expenditures, it apparently does not stimulate people's imaginations and motivate the members to take the time to develop a thorough systematic approach to the program.

Why does it work? What makes this an effective fund-raising technique? Many explanations have been offered, but four deserve mention here. First, and foremost, as was pointed out earlier, the churches have been far more effective than most leaders believe in teaching the concept of stewardship. This is one means of capitalizing on those teachings. Second, the venture usually includes all the characteristics of an ideal goal—specific, attainable, measurable, visible, unifying, and satisfying, with a terminal date and with the opportunity for a celebration of accomplishment at the end.

A third factor is the result of a major economic change during the past thirty-five years. In 1950 only a tiny fraction of the adult population had accumulated significant wealth. Today well over one-half of the adults in our society have substantial wealth. Much of the money raised in these campaigns comes from savings rather than from current income. The amount of money that Americans have in personal savings has doubled once every five or six years in recent decades.

Fourth, thousands of Protestant congregations are composed of an aging group of members. This is clearly the case with the majority of Presbyterian, United Methodist, Christian Church (Disciples of Christ), United Church of Canada, Episcopalian, and United Church of Christ congregations. As was emphasized earlier in this chapter, the segment of the population that has experienced the greatest increase in real income and that has enjoyed the largest increase in accumulated wealth has been the people born before 1930. These are the people most likely to be at worship on Sunday morning, these are the people with the greatest degree of denominational and congregational loyalty, and these are the people most likely to support this kind of "one big day."

Although there are dozens of systems that have been used to raise that very large sum of money on Miracle Sunday, three are most frequently utilized. The best is a carefully planned informational program defining the need, followed by a big inspirational dinner, followed by face-to-face calling to secure commitments before Miracle Sunday rolls around.

A second is a combination of letters to all members accompanied by personal visits on perhaps 20 percent of the member-households.

The third is simply a series of six or seven letters. In the six-letter format the first letter is from a highly respected and influential layperson to all members explaining the need and introducing the concept of Miracle Sunday. The second letter is from a different highly respected and influential layperson that expands on the contents of the first letter. The third letter is an inspirational message from the minister.

The fourth letter explains that to raise this very large amount of money it will be necessary to have several very generous gifts. Too often a leader in the 400-member congregation calculates, "Our goal is $120,000. We have 400 members. Therefore that means that if every member gives $300, we'll reach our goal."

That is *not* the way to raise $120,000 on that one big day. A more realistic statement might sound something like this: "If we're going to raise $120,000 in one day, we will need two gifts in the $10,000 bracket, three in the $5,000 to $10,000 range, six to eight of about $3,000 to $5,000, and at least eight or ten of more than $2,000 each." A safe assumption is that 80 percent of the money received on Miracle Sunday will come from 20 percent of the contributors. That fourth letter spells out the size of the largest gifts that must be received if that miracle is to come to pass. The pacesetters need to know in advance what the pace will be for this drive. Frequently the persons who may make large contributions will be visited personally.

The fifth letter arrives five to twelve days before Miracle Sunday and advises everyone that with their complete cooperation we will attain the goal; it may include the announcement that advance gifts equivalent to one-third the goal already have been received. The sixth letter goes out after Miracle Sunday, declares the event a victory, and thanks everyone for their cooperation.

Although it is not possible to answer all of the reader's questions in this brief essay, a half-dozen other considerations must be mentioned.

First, a critical factor is the purpose for which the money is to be used must not be a divisive issue. This is an excellent method of funding a need or cause which nearly everyone supports, but more important, no one strongly opposes!

Second, please do not confuse this with stewardship education. This is a fund-raising appeal designed on the assumption that your church already has done a better job of stewardship education than many believe to be the case.

Third, this is not suggested as an annual event! How often can you do this? It may be best to wait until after one-half of the members have joined since the last Miracle Sunday.

Fourth, take enough time. Usually ten to sixteen weeks is required between the date the governing body authorizes this venture and the day when Miracle Sunday rolls around. Take time to inform the members about the need and the process. Allow time for excitement to build. Give the members time to talk themselves into giving more than they originally planned to give. If you plan to send five or six letters before Miracle Sunday, allow six to eight weeks for that part of the process.

Fifth, in many parts of the continent the ideal Sunday is the second Sunday in May. In general, February, March, April, and May are better than November. The Sunday before Christmas or the Sunday after Christmas is an excellent choice, if the weather cooperates. In the Sunbelt the best time is shortly before the Snowbirds fly north. (Many Sunbelt congregations ask a Snowbird to chair this program.) The ideal Sunday is on the twenty-fifth or fiftieth or seventy-fifth or one-hundredth anniversary of the founding of your congregation.

Finally, what happens if you do not attain the goal? What happens if you ask for $100,000 and receive only $65,000? First, don't close the door too early. Second, you are now $65,000 better off than you were a month earlier. Third, thank

God. Fourth, thank your members. In other words, when you see a victory, call it a victory!

Bring in a Professional?

A lingering resistance still persists in many congregations to any proposal for second-mile giving. These churches may want to consider another alternative. This is to engage a professional to come in and direct the annual stewardship program. Although many members object to the cost (typically between 1.5 and 4 percent of the amount pledged), there are four major advantages to this system: (1) it broadens the base of financial support from among the membership, (2) it deepens the sense of stewardship, (3) it enables the church to continue with a unified budget, and (4) as a group these congregations have a per capita giving level at least 50 percent above the level of the other churches in that denominational family.

Finally, an increasing number of middle-sized congregations are turning to what once was thought to be an alternative open only to the large wealthy downtown churches. This is to encourage members to remember the church in their wills and tithe their estate, a concept that was presented earlier as part of the discussion on the capital-formation church in chapter 2.

Although there is no one formula that will solve all the financial problems of every middle-sized congregation, it is an important issue. If the finances are neglected, that can be one of the most effective means of subverting the basic purpose of the worshiping congregation and making institutional survival the number-one issue. That in turn undermines the essential nature of the middle-sized church for one of its distinctive characteristics is that it is sufficiently large to keep ministry ahead of survival on the daily agenda.

Notes

1. What Is the Middle-Sized Church?

1. Michael Rutter et al., *Fifteen Thousand Hours* (Cambridge, Mass.: Harvard University Press, 1979). See also James S. Coleman et al., *High School Achievement* (New York: Basic Books, 1982).

2. Roger G. Barker and Paul V. Gump, *Big School, Small School* (Stanford, Calif.: Stanford University Press, 1964).

3. Among the most useful of these studies are Ernest L. Boyer, *High School* (New York: Harper & Row, 1983); Theodore Sizer, *Horace's Compromise* (Boston: Houghton Mifflin, 1984); National Commission on Excellence in Education, *A Nation at Risk* (Washington: U. S. Department of Education, 1983); Mortimer Adler, *The Paideia Proposal* (New York: Macmillan, 1982); John I. Goodlad, *A Place Called School* (New York: McGraw-Hill, 1983); and Joan Lipsitz, *Successful Schools for Young Adolescents* (New Brunswick, N.J.: Transaction Books, 1983).

4. Thomas J. Peters and Robert H. Waterman, Jr., *In Search of Excellence* (New York: Harper & Row, 1982).

5. For a scholarly presentation of the thesis that the Pauline church tended to attract the upwardly mobile see Wayne A. Meeks, *The First Urban Christians* (New Haven: Yale University Press, 1982).

2. No Two Are Alike!

1. See Lyle E. Schaller, *Planning for Protestantism in Urban America* (Nashville: Abingdon Press, 1965), pp. 168-71, and Lyle E. Schaller, *Effective Church Planning* (Nashville: Abingdon Press, 1979), pp. 65-92, for a more detailed explanation of why place is so important to churches.

2. For a very useful conceptual framework for looking at these "graduates" see John Biersdorf, *Hunger for Experience* (New York: Seabury Press, 1976).

3. Perhaps the best book for whites who seek to become a racially inclusive congregation is James H. Davis and Woodie W. White, *Racial Transition in the Church* (Nashville: Abingdon Press, 1980). The writers offer sage counsel on how to develop and maintain a racially inclusive fellowship. A case can be made for the thesis that the most distinctive characteristic of the racially integrated church is that from the time of the Apostle Paul the Christian church has attracted the upwardly mobile who are not willing to accept the stratification of the population that society imposes on people who are interested in building a new world and who are filled with hope. Meeks, *The First Urban Christians.*

A new version of the racially integrated church is emerging on the Protestant scene. These congregations usually include fewer than 100 people at Sunday morning worship; a majority of the new members are young, urban professionals, born after 1950, and most of them are either never married or recently married and childless: the congregation meets in an old building in the central city or in an older suburb; race is rarely mentioned and almost always ignored as a distinctive factor; some members describe the congregation as "a country church in the city"; most of the new members are new to that community; the membership includes one or two or three interracial marriages and several intergenerational marriages; the current pastor has been serving that congregation for at least six or seven years; blacks are a highly visible and very active minority; a substantial proportion of the members display a strong interest in social justice and causes such as peace or racial integration; a significant number of the members had experienced unhappy or unrewarding times in other churches and are enthusiastic in their affirmation of this congregation; the choir director is a patient individual who understands the distinction between repetition and drill; the congregation does not adhere to a rigid time schedule; it is clear that the members both give and receive energy from one another; and for many newcomers this congregation is a great place to meet and make new friends.

For those seeking a case study of a congregation organized around social action see Jeffrey K. Hadden and Charles F. Longino, Jr., *Gideon's Gang* (New York: Pilgrim Press, 1974).

5. The Awkward-Sized Church

1. For further elaboration on a ministry of music see Lyle E. Schaller, "Music in the Large Church," *Choristers Guild Letters*, March 1980, pp. 123-25.

2. See Lyle E. Schaller, *The Tensions of Reapportionment* (New York: National Council of Churches, 1965).

3. Clark Kerr, *The Uses of the University*, 3rd ed. (Cambridge, Mass.: Harvard University Press, 1982).

4. For additional suggestions on developing and managing large groups see Lyle E. Schaller, *Effective Church Planning* (Nashville: Abingdon Press, 1979), pp. 17-63; Lyle E. Schaller, "What Holds a Class Together?" *Church*

71227

School Today, Winter 1982-83; and Lyle E. Schaller, "The Rule of Forty," *The Christian Ministry*, September 1983.

5. For an elaboration of the concept of the transformations leader see James MacGregor Burns, *Leadership* (New York: Harper & Row, 1978).

6. Financing the Middle-Sized Church

1. The studies of Muncie, Indiana, indicated that in 1978 the average working-class family contributed 3.3 percent of the family income to religious causes compared to 1.6 percent in 1924. Theodore Caplow et al., *Middletown Families* (Minneapolis: University of Minnesota Press, 1982), pp. 267-68. See also Douglas W. Johnson, *The Tithe* (Nashville: Abingdon Press, 1984), and Joe W. Walker, *Money in the Church* (Nashville: Abingdon Press, 1982).

2. In 1970 the average annual income of Americans age sixty-five and over was 104 percent of the average for the total population. In 1978 that figure was 106 percent. Two-thirds of the elderly own their own homes. Michael D. Hurd and John B. Shoven, *The Economic Status of the Elderly* (New York: National Bureau of Economic Research, 1982).

3. For a discussion of one of the most effective approaches to capital funds appeals see David Owen, "State-of-the-Art Panhandling," *Harper's*, August 1982.

4. Douglas W. Johnson et al., *North American Interchurch Study* (New York: National Council of Churches, 1971).

5. Joseph Veroff et al., *The Inner American* (New York: Basic Books, 1981).